Praise for *The Sales Development Playbook*

"*The Sales Development Playbook* is chock-full of actionable ideas, tips, and real-life examples of creating a super high-performing SDR program. One of only a handful true experts, Trish shares a lifetime of knowledge and experience. It's a must-read for anyone who manages sales development teams."

—Bob Perkins
Founder and Chairman of AA-ISP

"People get hung up on the wrong questions around sales development: templates, tools, and tricks. *The Sales Development Playbook* asks and answers the right questions. If you're looking to increase qualified pipeline, read this book."

—Mark Roberge
Chief Revenue Officer, HubSpot
author of *The Sales Acceleration Formula*

"Finally, a single resource and starting point to build out a new sales development team or BOOST an existing one. Trish Bertuzzi makes it simple with *The Sales Development Playbook*. There's a reason for the rocket on the cover of the book – do these six things right and your team's revenues will take off!"

—Lori Richardson
Founder and CEO, Score More Sales

"If you want more revenue, read this book. Trish has managed to give away ALL of the secrets. Years of trial and error for sales development strategies all packed into one book. If you're looking for research, examples, and bold thinking, look no further."

—Steve Richard
Chief Revenue Officer, ExecVision.io

D0089424

"Sales development continues to be the winning strategy for opening new accounts, building pipeline, and driving growth. Anyone - CEOs, VPs, and Front-Line Managers - trying to master sales development needs this smart, detailed book."

—Natasha Sekkat
VP of Sales Development, VMTurbo

"There is no one more knowledgeable than Trish when it comes to the fundamentals of building Sales Development teams. Hands down. This book is a must-read for anyone who interested in building a productive, scalable, and highly successful SDR function."

—Devon McDonald
Partner, OpenView Venture Partners

"If you're looking to lead Inside Sales or Sales Development, the very first thing you should do is read this book! Trish, the self-proclaimed Queen of Inside Sales, has earned her title."

—Chad Burmeister
Senior Director, Global Sales Development, RingCentral

"To build new pipeline and accelerate growth, master the six elements outlined in this book. It truly is the Sales Development bible."

—Jill Konrath
Author of *Agile Selling*,
SNAP Selling and *Selling to Big Companies*

"If you're serious about building new pipeline and growing your company, this is the most detailed, honest, and useful book ever written."

—Pete Gracey
CEO and Co-Founder, QuotaFactory

THE
SALES
DEVELOPMENT
PLAYBOOK

Build Repeatable Pipeline and Accelerate Growth with Inside Sales

TRISH BERTUZZI

This publication may not be reproduced, stored in a retrieval system, or transmitted in whole or in part, in any form or by any means, electronic, mechanical, photocopying, recording, or otherwise, except as permitted under Section 107 or 108 of the 1976 United States Copyright Act, without the prior written permission of Trish Bertuzzi. Requests for permission should be addressed to Trish Bertuzzi, The Bridge Group, Inc., PO Box 863, Hudson, MA 01749 or emailed to info@bridgegroupinc.com.

LIBRARY OF CONGRESS CATALOGING-IN-PUBLICATION DATA
Bertuzzi, Trish. The Sales Development Playbook: build repeatable pipeline and accelerate growth with inside sales / by Trish Bertuzzi; foreword by Ken Krogue.

Limit of Liability/Disclaimer of Warranty: While the publisher and authors have used their best efforts in preparing this book, they make no representations or warranties with respect to the accuracy or completeness of the contents of this book and specifically disclaim any implied warranties of merchantability or fitness for a particular purpose. No warranty may be created or extended by sales representatives or written sales materials. The advice and strategies contained herein may not be suitable for your situation. Neither the publisher nor the authors shall be liable for any loss of profit or other commercial damages, including but not limited to special, incidental, consequential or other damages.

First Edition
ISBN 978-0-692-62203-2

10 9 8 7 6 5 4 3 2 1

Dedicated to my son Matt without whom there would be no business, brand, or book.

CONTENTS

FOREWORD

This is the first successful thing I've written since my head-on collision with a big truck destroyed my Chevy pickup and put me in an ambulance on the 2nd day of September 2015. My previous attempt—on what is supposed to be my weekly column on Forbes—got taken down in four hours. It wasn't good.

Trish has been patient. Her kind but consistent follow-through, some coaching from my former Forbes editor Tom Post, and the patience of my family, staff, and friends have helped pull me back to the world of writing.

Thanks, Trish. That's what friends do. I have a long way to go, but at least I now have a bigger truck!

I've known Trish for a long time. In internet years, it's almost a lifetime. I "met" Trish years ago by hanging out in her Inside Sales Experts group on LinkedIn. I was very intrigued by her discussion topics, so I joined in and asked a few weighty questions and she responded. Pretty soon, we had a consistent interaction going and took our conversation offline . . . to the phone. I could tell immediately she was a master, while at the same time a warm, funny, fiery person who loves what she does.

We were soon both speaking at an event, and she was the first person I had to track down and meet face to face. She ran up and gave me such a big hug. Then I saw her present, and I knew she was world class. She completely owns the stage. The people love her.

That's Trish.

Then we became friends. We talked about blogging and how powerful it was, how it took a long time to have the impact we wanted. Like a flywheel slowly building momentum. Then our blogs took off as our budding profession became an industry that changed the landscape of business-to-business sales and marketing.

We would debate the rise and fall of trends. I saw the rise of sales 2.0 very early, and she called out the death of BANT as a qualification methodology. Trish covers BANT (budget, authority, need, and timing) and its replacement in detail in part 1. I remember she said that "putting budget first is like asking for W2 forms on the first date!" She set the stage for ANUM, the qualification model I built at my company InsideSales.com, and her trademark one liners once again led the way for industry change.

That's Trish.

I'm an old football coach. Sales, as a profession, is very closely aligned with competitive athletics. Really great coaches have a playbook that they continually refine and improve, but it's always based on a foundation, the blocking and tackling of success. That's what this book is. It gives you the system while it teaches you to test and improve through iteration.

My other hobby is military strategy. Throughout the centuries of warfare, taking the high ground first would win you the battle. Keep maneuvering to take the high ground first, and you win the war.

Sales development, or the art and science of finding leads and qualifying opportunities, is the high ground of sales. When it's all said and done, it's all about the leads. That's where you need to focus—where the most leverage is.

The Sales Development Playbook leads with strategy and then walks you through specialization, recruiting and retaining people, execution, and leadership. This is the playbook for how to succeed today.

Every time I've seen Trish for the last two to three years, I've looked her in the eye and said, "You need to write a book!" She would say, "I know, I know already! I'm getting that from all directions!" And every time she sees me, she coaches me on how to improve our organization and our playbook at InsideSales.com.

After reading this book, I know it will help you succeed, help your company grow, and change our industry.

And all I can say is it's about dang time! ☺

KEN KROGUE
Founder & President, InsideSales.com
Provo, Utah

INTRODUCTION

RAISE YOUR HAND if your company needs more new customers. I suspect your hand is (figuratively) up. Every business wants to grow. Because you're reading this book, chances are you don't want to just grow. You want high growth, explosive growth, the kind of growth that weather satellites can see from space.

Now, raise your hand if prospects are falling over each other in a mad dash to enter the top of your sales funnel. If your account executives are already swigging Gatorade, taking orders, and closing six-figure deals with a sixty-second sales process, this probably isn't the book for you. If you want to build repeatable sales pipeline and have a make-it-happen mindset, then read on.

If you're a CEO or if you run a department of sales or marketing, you may be wondering how you can accelerate revenue growth from so-so to stellar. I'm sure you have a fantastic product and great sales team, but perhaps there just isn't enough activity at the top of the funnel.

You may already be running a sales development group but have a nagging suspicion that somewhere, lurking unseen, inefficiencies are dragging down productivity. Or maybe you've been handed the reins of a team and are overwhelmed at where to begin. In either case, this book is here to help.

The success of any company is directly linked to how effectively it acquires new pipeline. Account managers can't grow accounts and service reps can't support accounts without net new customers. Not to put too much pressure on you, but everyone at your company's livelihood depends on how well you build new pipeline. It's just that important. For you personally, success with sales development isn't just a stepping stone in your career; it's a giant leap forward.

To skyrocket growth, I believe *sales development* is the answer. This book encapsulates my three decades of practical, hands-on experience. At my sales consulting company, The Bridge Group, Inc., my team and I have designed and implemented hundreds of sales development teams. From startup, to scale-up, growth, and global enterprise, we've worked with more than 250 technology, life science, and service companies.

Here is how I define sales development:

A specialized role focused on the frontend of the sales process—qualifying inbound leads and/or conducting outbound prospecting—to generate sales pipeline

I was compelled to write this book because of a major problem I'm seeing. There's a fundamental misunderstanding of how to "do" sales development. Again and again, I see Company B copying and pasting bits and pieces of what Company A is doing (or, more accurately, *what it appears it is doing*) and failing to maximize its own results. From the outside, it's easy to see that a given company (or competitor) has sales development. But it is next to impossible to see *why*, *how*, and *if* that approach is appropriate for you.

I've identified six elements for sales development success (see figure I.1).

Figure I.1 – The six elements

My decades of experience as seller, inside sales director, VP of sales, and business consultant have led me to these six elements. I wish I could tell you that one beautiful New England morning, looking out over the lake, I saw the pink light of dawn and inspiration struck. But it didn't happen like that. The six elements are the byproduct of years of trial and error, witnessing mistakes, decoding success, and working hard with hundreds of smart, hungry client companies. This is a proven system that I've deployed with companies you've heard of to refocus and redouble growth as well as with companies I'm confident you will be hearing about.

Perhaps you're already excelling at some of the six elements today. You can achieve lift-off if you execute one or two well. Good strategy and good recruiting, for instance, will deliver some return. You can even produce respectable results by excelling at three or four elements. But if you truly want to nail sales development—if you want to be a legend in building repeatable pipeline and leading a world-class team—all six elements need to be mastered.

Sales development is an "overnight sensation" thirty years in the making. And I'm thrilled that this day has finally arrived. My business card might say "President and Chief Strategist," but helping companies excel at reaching prospects and generating new pipeline is my passion. In my writing, speaking, and consulting, I've seen it time and time again: the companies that master each of the six elements are the ones that generate *truly* stellar results.

The strategies, stories, examples, and tools you'll encounter in these pages will take your ability to build pipeline to the next level. Thank *you* for making the time to take this journey with me.

Remember, your career, your culture, and everyone else's livelihood is depending on you. Let's not waste one more minute.

DEFINING OUR TERMS

You may know these acronyms already, but just so we're all aligned, I'd like to define the terms I'll use throughout the book.

▶ *Sales development reps* (or SDRs) are responsible for the front end of the sales process. They either set introductory meetings or generate qualified opportunities for sales partners.

▶ *Inbound sales development reps* (often called BDRs, LDRs, or similar) are responsible for inbound lead qualification in response to marketing programs.

▶ *Outbound sales development reps* (often called ADRs, MDRs, or similar) are responsible for outbound prospecting.

▶ *Account executives* carry a revenue quota. Also called territory managers, sales executives, or similar, they convert opportunities into closed business. For our purposes, this can include inside (phone-based) or field (road-warrior) sales reps.

Throughout this book, I've tapped the wisdom of forty-one practitioners and subject matter experts. As you well know, sales leaders change jobs *often*. All of the titles of the people mentioned are as of this writing.

PART 1

STRATEGY

The essence of strategy is choosing what not to do.
MICHAEL E. PORTER

Successful sales development means choosing the right goals, plans, and actions for your unique market dynamics.

In this section, I'll cover:
- ► The case for sales development
- ► Aligning your model to your market and sales process
- ► Critical success factors: reporting, expectations, and handoff

CHAPTER 1

SELLING IN THE 21ST CENTURY

TWO MAJOR WAVES ARE COLLIDING. They are changing the way business-to-business (B2B) selling and buying are done.

The first wave is the exponential growth in the number of ideas, options, and solutions available for (and marketed to) your prospects. Prospects are under siege. They're drowning in a sea of *could do*. Sellers are publishing new and often-contradictory "thought leadership" pieces at a startling rate. In response, prospects have developed a bias for the status quo. It just seems safer to stick with the way things are.

> *Successful selling today requires cutting through the spam cannonade of emails and rising above the white noise of half-hearted prospecting.*

The companies that win today are those that are willing to reach out, stand out, and point out flaws in status quo thinking. Your prospects are primarily concerned with how you can help them build a better business. Selling isn't interruption or trickery. It is, at its heart, about service.

The second wave in play concerns the number and diversity of people involved in purchasing decisions. The "buyer" has become the "buying unit" and is quickly growing into the "buying battalion." It is getting more and more difficult to draw clean lines between *decision makers, influencers,* and *users.* Just about any single sale process seems to require dozens of *yeses* and risks running aground in the face of a single *no*. While sales cycles haven't elongated exponentially, the amount of effort required to win a single sale has.

As a result, account executives (those reps who close sales) increasingly lack the time—and often the desire—to focus on building new sales pipelines. They argue that their time is better spent advancing and closing opportunities. "I'm busy doing demos, drafting proposals, and chasing contracts. I'm not prospecting because I just don't have the bandwidth," they say. Enter the sales development function.

Sales Development

The sales development role is our best response to the realities detailed above. If both prospects and account executives are *crazy busy*, we need a dedicated role for executing top-of-the-funnel activity that is purpose built for generating new pipeline. For many companies, the sales development reps are the first line of human contact with prospects. When performing the role well, they can also be the best opportunity to spark curiosity and generate interest.

You may be thinking, I already understand how this role can make life easier for my account executives, but what's in it for my business?

The value of a sales development effort is measured by increased won business per account executive and/or accelerated new customer acquisition.

That's it. It's all about the benjamins: more pipeline, more revenue, and more new customers. If you increase lead conversion rates, but you aren't closing more business, what's the point? Similarly, if your account executives are having twice as many introductory meetings, but you aren't gaining more new customers, you're just spinning your wheels. Effective sales development is about ratcheting up your ability to build new pipeline and accelerate revenue growth. Period.

After years of second-class status and often derogatory labels—*Oh, that's telemarketing* or *That's just teleprospecting*—the role has finally come into its own. Venture capitalists, CEOs, and boards of advisors now pay as much attention to pipeline reviews as they do forecast reviews. Success in sales development means accepting the two realities I detailed above and committing to excellence through a sustained focus on the top of the funnel.

Scott Maxwell is managing partner of OpenView Venture Partners, a venture capital fund. I asked him how he views the sales development role as he thinks through making investment decisions. "Every company that we invest in either has or will have a sales development team. Unless the price point of the product is so low that it's impossible to justify, sales development is a necessary ingredient. It's kind of like having a CFO."

As I shared in the introduction, sales development is the most effective way to get in front of more prospects and drive more pipeline. But it is no easy task. There are six critical elements you must master to get the amazing results you deserve.

The Six Elements

This book is divided into six parts. Each focuses on a specific element of revenue acceleration with sales development (see Figure 1.1).

Figure 1.1 – The Six Elements

Part 1: Strategy shares a framework for thinking about how to align your sales development model with your specific market dynamics and buyer's journey. After reading part 1, you'll have the criteria to determine your model and be fully versed in the critical success factors.

9

Part 2: Specialization presents stories of innovative companies applying new thinking and taking their groups to the next level. You'll learn about segmenting your prospect universe, specializing roles, and how it all comes together.

In Part 3: Recruiting, I offer a roadmap for hiring with urgency and attracting top talent. Recruiting tactics, compensation, and a bulletproof hiring process are presented in great detail.

Part 4: Retention goes deep on the stuff that never seems to get enough consideration: engaging, developing, and motivating people. These chapters are filled with actionable advice on everything from coaching to building career paths.

In Part 5: Execution, I switch gears and present strategies and examples for onboarding, crafting buyer-based messaging, and designing effective outreach. You'll get dozens of ideas on everything from methodology to creating amazing voicemail and email messages.

And finally, Part 6: Leadership gives actionable advice on what it takes to lead sales development today. There's a lot to learn about quota setting, measuring what matters, and acceleration technologies, so those are covered in depth.

You don't have to read every sentence in this book to see results. Perhaps your company isn't ready for Part 2: Specialization *today*. Or perhaps Part 1: Strategy isn't within your span of control *yet*. Each part of this book is more tapas than six-course meal. But to truly master sales development, you're going to have to spend time with each part.

Understanding all six elements and adapting for your specific market dynamics is the only way to achieve wildly successful results. Let's meet two companies that have done just that.

$70M and $7M: Two Companies' Journeys

Acquia helps many of the world's biggest brands deliver digital experiences with greater agility and speed. It is one of Boston's fastest-growing companies, boasting five-year growth of more than 4,900 percent. An incredibly strong marketing engine brought it to nearly $70M in revenues.

But the company wanted more. To further accelerate growth, it determined to go outbound with sales development.

From rep to manager and head of worldwide inside sales, Tom Murdock has seen Acquia's journey firsthand. Tom shared that in eighteen months, Acquia built an outbound team focused on generating qualified opportunities and grew it to thirty reps. Tom described the following results:

- ▶ Outbound SDRs have pipeline targets of ~$700K per rep per quarter
- ▶ The new business growth rate nearly doubled after adding the outbound component

In the process, Acquia did something very unique. Most companies will start reps as inbound SDRs, qualifying inbound leads, and promote them into an outbound role after they've proven themselves. (Note: I'll cover both role specialization and career path in great detail in parts 2 and 4, respectively.) Acquia chose to reverse that. Tom shared their thinking: "We found that our inbound leads are very familiar with our company, our products, and our competitors. Our mentality is to put the best leads in front of our best pipeline generators." For Acquia, that meant starting reps as outbound prospectors and promoting top performers into the inbound team.

The point to notice isn't how specifically Acquia implemented its group but rather that "how everyone else does it" didn't dictate its approach. Acquia was willing to build a sales development strategy based entirely on the realities of its specific market. That's why it continues to be one of the highest-growth companies in the technology space.

Listrak, which provides a digital marketing platform for retailers, took a very different tack. CEO Ross Kramer had grown his company to $7M in revenues with a sales model that had account executives owning both prospecting and closing responsibilities. Ross's account executives were "more than happy to drink the inbound Kool-Aid and assume that prospecting meant only calling people who had filled out a form." The problem was that Listrak wasn't generating enough inbound inquiries to meet its pipeline targets.

Much like Acquia, Listrak realized that accelerating revenue growth required targeted outbound. To support the company's new focus on the top of the funnel, Ross built two new teams. The first team sets introductory meetings for the account executives. The second is tasked with finding prospects for the *meeting setters* to call. "I have a colleague who uses the term *creative avoidance*. Noodling on your data inside of CRM is a great way to avoid making calls, as is flipping through people on LinkedIn," shared Ross. "That's why we do a hard separation. The people making the calls don't update the data. They're not responsible for finding the next lead or finding a better contact." The strategy is paying off:

▶ Ross has grown his company's revenues more than 400 percent.

▶ He attributes more than 65 percent of that revenue to the sales development effort.

As you can see, Tom and Ross took very different paths along their sales development journeys. They both made the decision to break the sales process into prospecting (SDRs) and closing (AE roles).From there, however, their paths diverged. While both built and scaled sales development, Acquia and Listrak innovated based on their unique market dynamics. I can't emphasize strongly enough that reality on the ground, not the case study available online, should drive strategy.

In the rest of this book, I'll share strategies, stories, examples, and tools to help you implement the right sales development approach for your market. By embracing the six elements, you'll be on your way to accelerating your company's growth and your personal career trajectory.

Let's get started.

CHAPTER 2

CONSIDER THE FIVE WHYS

IN 1925, EDWARD STRONG, PHD, a professor of applied psychology at Stanford University, made the concept of AIDA famous. The four steps in AIDA stand for attention, interest, desire, and action. AIDA is a convenient framework for thinking about the stages buyers pass through when making a simple business-to-business (B2B) purchase.

But for those of us with high-ticket products and complex sales processes, AIDA doesn't quite fit. To be successful today, your sales process and sales development strategy must align with the way your prospects think (often called the buyer's journey). I've built a five-step framework for thinking about the modern B2B buying process. I call it *The Five Whys* (see figure 2.1).

Figure 2.1 – The Five Whys

The Five Whys are questions that prospects ask themselves along the way in a complex B2B purchase. As we walk through *The Five Whys*, put yourself in your prospects' shoes. Remember, every vendor is squawking and screeching trying to gain prospect attention. To stay ahead of all those competitors, you have to take their reality into consideration.

In figure 2.2, the first column reflects the *why* stage. Column two (Prospect Before) is where prospects start when you begin communicating with them. Column three (Prospect After) is where they hopefully end up if all goes according to plan. The final column is how the Prospect After stage aligns to a traditional sales process.

	PROSPECT BEFORE	PROSPECT AFTER	CORRESPONDING SALES STAGE
WHY LISTEN?	Crazy busy	Curious	Introductory meeting
WHY CARE?	Curious	Interested	Discovery call
WHY CHANGE?	Interested	Active	Pipeline opportunity
WHY YOU?	Active	Committed to you	Forecast opportunity
WHY NOW?	Committed to you	Committed to now	A win

Figure 2.2 – The Five Whys expanded

Looking at the sales process this way, we can appreciate just how much effort it takes to move a company from *prospect* to *customer*. We can also appreciate what a journey prospects have to make from "unexpected sales call" to "this is something I want to pursue" and finally to "replacing the status quo."

In a transactional sale (think high-volume, low-touch, and quick sales cycle), all five gates might be crossed in days or weeks. In an enterprise sale (think complex, high-ticket, and long sales cycle), it might take quarters. And if selling to the Fortune 500, just crossing from *WHY YOU* to *WHY NOW* can seem to take a lifetime. (I'm looking at you, purchasing departments!)

There's one piece I want you to pay special attention to. In figure 2.3, notice just how distinct the first two *whys* (Listen and Care) are from the last three (Change, You, and Now).

The final three *whys* (Change, You, and Now) are about gaining commitment and closing a sale. They are the domain of account executives, and, as such, we won't be discussing them further. But take another look at the first two *whys* (Listen and Care). These two are about opening doors and sparking interest. At first glance, they might seem similar, but there's quite a bit of distance between the two.

	PROSPECT BEFORE	PROSPECT AFTER
WHY LISTEN?	Crazy busy	Curious
WHY CARE?	Curious	Interested
WHY CHANGE?	Interested	Active
WHY YOU?	Active	Committed to you
WHY NOW?	Committed to you	Committed to now

Figure 2.3 – Prospect Before & Prospect After

The essence of sales development strategy is deciding how far down *The Five Whys* your reps can and should take prospects. Where to draw the line is a decision that you'll have to make and likely revisit as your team grows. Here's how to get started.

WHY LISTEN & WHY CARE

Okay, we've established that *WHY LISTEN* and *WHY CARE* are the domain of sales development. But what exactly should you expect your team to be closing on? Sales development teams can be tasked with either a) setting introductory meetings or b) generating qualified opportunities. We'll cover the difference in more detail in chapter 3. But for now, I tend to think of the introductory meetings model as addressing the *WHY LISTEN* stage only. Teams that address both *WHY LISTEN* and *WHY CARE* are generating qualified opportunities.

Sales development is a tough job. Reps have to reach often unsuspecting (a.k.a. cold) prospects and get them to stop what they are doing and listen. That's miles easier said than done. Think of all the people competing for your attention on a daily basis: your family, your employees, your peers, your boss, and countless sales reps trying to get "just twenty minutes on your calendar to discuss your strategy for blah blah." Regardless of what you're shooting for—

an introductory meeting, technology demo, or fully qualified opportunity—your reps' first hurdle is to arouse curiosity and get prospects to *listen*.

Let's assume mission accomplished and the prospect is curious. Now, onto the second hurdle. Your reps have to demonstrate an understanding of their prospects' industries, priorities, and challenges. They need to shine a spotlight on gaps in the prospects' current approach and bring them around to your way of thinking. In short, your reps have to evolve curiosity into interest while at the same time qualifying for fit.

Remember the two companies we met in the previous chapter? Let's take a look at how Acquia's and Listrak's approaches map to *The Five Whys* (see figure 2.4).

	WHY STAGES	PROSPECT AFTER	MODEL
ACQUIA	Why Listen? + Why Care?	Interested	Qualified opportunities
LISTRAK	Why Listen?	Curious	Introductory meetings

Figure 2.4 – Acquia's & Listrak's Whys

Acquia's account executives have a requirement for qualified opportunities. As such, the sales development teams must bring prospects through the WHY LISTEN and WHY CARE gates before handoff. Listrak's AEs, on the other hand, have a requirement for more at-bats. Their SDRs are setting introductory meetings. This involves addressing just WHY LISTEN before handing off to the closing rep.

The point here is not to say that one model is universally better than the other. In fact, from my sales development research, I know that there are nearly the same numbers of companies with *introductory meeting* as *qualified opportunity* models. The argument I'm making is that the starting point for sales development shouldn't be which model you, your CEO, or your board *prefers*, but which model best addresses the realities of your specific market. I'll help you think through that decision and its implications in the next chapter.

CHAPTER 3

<hr>

LET REQUIREMENTS GUIDE YOUR MODEL

MUCH LIKE GOLDILOCKS AND THE PORRIDGE, your model needs to be "just right" for your organization. Figuring this out early will save you from account executives' complaints such as "Those leads weren't qualified enough. They aren't worth my time" or "My SDR isn't passing enough meetings. What are they doing all day?"

Effective sales development means maximizing the productivity of *both* the SDR and the AE teams. As we discussed in the last chapter, there are two main models in play: *setting introductory meetings* and *generating qualified opportunities*.

Don't believe anyone who says you should consider only one or the other. There are hundreds of companies successfully setting introductory meetings. Hundreds more are productively generating qualified opportunities. And more still are utilizing a blended approach for different products, market segments, or territories. Let your unique requirements guide your model. To help you along the way, here are a few general principles on when each model is most effective.

► **SETTING INTRODUCTORY MEETINGS:** Let's be clear on the realities here. The meetings being set here are *introductory*—from the Latin "introda," meaning *not ready to buy yet*. (Kidding!) This can include face-to-face meetings or a discovery phone call. With introductory meetings, prospects have a sense of your overall value

17

proposition but haven't been qualified as to their readiness or ability to move forward.

▶ **GENERATING QUALIFIED OPPORTUNITIES:** Qualified opportunities differ in that they are, well, qualified. The rep is still closing on a meeting or call but has a) moved the prospect from curiosity into interest and b) vetted that the prospect meets or exceeds a minimum threshold of "sales-worthiness." We'll discuss more on qualification criteria later in this chapter.

Introductory Meetings

One of the biggest mistakes I see companies make is setting internal expectations using introductory meeting metrics (quantity) and then requiring opportunity-level qualification (quality). This seemingly innocuous misstep often ends in total disaster. "Qualified introductory meetings" is an oxymoron. If your sales development process and expectations are at cross purposes, account executives will lose faith in the team, your SDRs will burn out, your culture will sour, and your group will fail to deliver.

As I mentioned earlier, I don't consider one model universally better, or more effective, than the other. I do believe that in certain situations, one is likely *more appropriate* than the other. Here's my rule of thumb.

You should deploy an introductory meeting model when the market for your product is immature and/or when your account executives need more at-bats.

Let me give you an example. Today, customer relationship management (CRM) software is a mature market. Most (if not all) technology-enabled companies already have a solution in place. Those companies have existing contracts with future renewal dates, and the thought of changing providers sounds like a major hassle. In this instance, if your SDRs are setting introductory meetings for the AEs, you're just wasting everyone's time.

The prospects will be frustrated, thinking, "Why are they trying to close me? I told them we're under contract for another year." The account executive will be frustrated, thinking, "Why am I here? They have zero chance of buying this quarter." And the SDR will be frustrated, thinking, "I'm setting all these meetings like I'm supposed to. It isn't my fault they aren't closing." This is totally the wrong model in this instance.

Compare that to the market for a predictive lead scoring solution. That market is still immature, as the concept *itself* is new. Vendors are faced with doing the work of educating the market on the problem they solve. Rather than qualify themselves out of a meeting, sales development reps should be closing on meetings at full speed in this category.

In terms of qualification for introductory meetings, you can't get much beyond *right profile*, *right person*, and *right high-level pain*.

If your SDRs are booking meetings with the right types of companies, the right people within them, and the prospects are at least curious about addressing a potential pain point, then the reps have done their jobs well.

Below, you'll find two types of requests that account executives often make to their sales development counterparts. The first focuses on right profile, right person, and right pain. The second is an unreasonably high bar (but a far-from-uncommon request).

▶ **REASONABLE:** A meeting with a director in the "quality operations" department at a $500M+ pharmaceutical company who has high-level pain around collaboration in bringing new drugs to market. Right profile, right person, right pain: *check, check,* and *check*. These types of meetings will be plentiful and will set your AEs up for success.

▶ **ABSURD:** A meeting with the entire "quality operations" buying team at Pfizer after they have acknowledged this is a top three priority this quarter, have earmarked budget, and have shared their detailed purchase timeframe. This is what we in sales call a "bluebird." The likelihood of finding one of these—let alone multiple monthly—is tiny. We are looking for the intersection of ideal for the AE and feasible for the SDR.

In an immature market, the number one challenge your SDRs face is to arouse curiosity around a business issue that potentially hasn't even been recognized yet. Sales development should be teeing up introductory meetings so that the account executive can do the work of educating the prospect and developing that curiosity into interest. If you're selling a disruptive solution, asking BANT (budget, authority, need, and timing) types of questions makes no sense. There isn't going to be a budget set aside for problems that prospects don't know they have.

Think about qualifying for "authority" for a moment. Emerging problems don't have neat and tidy roles built to address them. Your reps should be arousing curiosity and setting meetings—not qualifying your company *out* of deals.

Perhaps this way of thinking about it will help. *What's your budget for a new smartphone?* You probably have a ballpark number in mind, as I'm fairly certain that the mobile phone market is highly mature. *Now, what's your budget for a trip to Mars?* Feels like an odd question, right? Perhaps that's because you aren't sure you need or want to make the voyage. I should probably spend some time convincing you that Earth isn't what it used to be before I ask if you have decision-making authority to book inter-planetary travel.

The second case for the introductory meeting model is when account executives are suffering from *empty calendar syndrome.* This one is easy. If your sales team is screaming for more "at-bats," then break glass and set meetings. Conversion rates, qualification criteria, and cost per meeting all go out the window when your account executives' calendars are anemic. Setting introductory meetings in this scenario is your go-to.

I've never met a sales organization that quibbled over degree of qualification when AEs were starving to have more conversations with prospects. This is often the case for young companies that are just going to market or established companies that are launching new products (or even taking existing products into new market segments). In these cases, setting introductory meetings is an effective mechanism for rapid learning. The process would follow these four steps:

1. **HYPOTHESIZE:** Build a hypothesis of which companies need your solution. Develop baseline messaging and identify target prospects.

2. **TEST:** Schedule as many introductory meetings as possible. SDRs and account executives test messaging before, during, and after meetings.

3. **ITERATE:** Based on learning, iterate on both the target profile and the message.

4. **REPEAT:** Rinse and repeat, learning more and more each time.

Here's an example of how this plays out. Tom Turner is an executive who has built and scaled sales development teams. Tom served as vice president of marketing for Q1Labs from its early days through an acquisition by IBM. Today, Tom is back in the startup world as EVP of sales and marketing for BitSight Technologies. I asked him how he thinks through the appropriateness of *meetings versus opportunities*. "You have to have your ideal prospect and best resonating messages nailed down first. Introductory meetings help you do that. Once you have both of those, that's when you should shift focus towards qualified opportunities."

Tom's point is that *degree of qualification* and *conversion rates* are important concerns, but only after your account executives have full pipelines and numerous active opportunities to work. That is the tipping point.

Qualified Opportunities

To clarify, a qualified opportunity is still a meeting or call, but one where the account has reached a qualification threshold. At some level, this means:

▶ A problem has been identified

▶ A potential solution was introduced

▶ And the prospect has committed to a next step

It sounds so simple, doesn't it? As you well know, arousing curiosity, generating interest, and getting prospects to open up about their priorities is about as easy as potty-training a coyote. The days of executives picking up their phones and patiently answering intrusive sales questions are gone. Your reps have to engage multiple prospects, speak intelligently to each prospect's specific needs, and create value in return for the right to have their questions answered.

The key to success with generating qualified opportunities lies in ensuring that your sales development team and your sales organization are on the same page when it comes to the qualification criteria.

Let's go back to a concept mentioned earlier, BANT: *budget, authority, need,* and *timing.* For many years, BANT was the criterion by which all opportunities were measured. Sales development teams would connect with prospects and immediately begin to grill them. They might ask:

▶ Are you aware of any initiatives ongoing or planned for establishing or expanding your [. . .] systems?

▶ How will you be involved in the decision-making process for this project?

▶ Have you established a timeframe to make a decision?

▶ What is the status of the funding for this project?

▶ What is your approximate budget?

▶ What is the most appropriate next step at this point?

Sometimes reps would even ask questions in the exact BANT order, leaving prospects wondering: *Wait! Was I just BANTed?* For most organizations, this approach is past its prime. I tend to think of it this way:

Qualifying for BANT is like going on a first date and asking to see a credit report.

Yes, you want to know if your future partner is a financial nightmare or on solid footing, but come on. Too much, too soon.

Qualification 2.0

There remains one redeeming aspect of BANT. It's easy to remember. No, seriously. Don't underestimate the value of a catchy acronym. If you've built a non-BANT qualification framework, go grab an account executive and see if he or she can recite each piece correctly. Dollars to donuts, he or she will miss something. In working with clients, I've built a qualification methodology I call PACT: *pain, authority, consequence,* and *target profile.* Let's take them each in turn.

- ▶ **PAIN:** Not every company has a need for your product or service (*the horror!*). And some that do need to buy from you stubbornly refuse to admit it. You can have access and a good relationship with the CEO of a Fortune 500 company, but if her team doesn't agree that you solve a pressing business issue, you're dead in the water. Pain matters.

- ▶ **AUTHORITY:** You likely have multiple decision makers involved in your sale. Reps need to understand the role that each person plays. Remember my earlier comment that any sale requires dozens of yeses and runs aground in the face of a single no? Don't just think "sign on the dotted line" authority. You are looking for people who can get an organization to move. That isn't always reflected in a title.

- ▶ **CONSEQUENCE:** Prospects are human—with all the misbehaviors and contradictions that entails. Plenty of companies have suffered with acknowledged pain for years. Their biggest issue is fear that the cure will hurt worse than the illness. You need to dig for the implications of *not acting.* An organization that isn't in motion is much harder to move than one that has already realized the consequences of inaction.

> ▶ **TARGET PROFILE:** This one is all about confirming fit and
> identifying red flags. Are there technical, cultural, or internal political
> issues that will kill the deal? There is no point in wasting an account
> executive's time on the false promise of a *no-way, no-how*
> opportunity.

PACT is useful for 90 percent of companies with opportunity-generating teams. I will make one small amendment for a certain situation. *If you're selling into a mature market and attempting to displace an existing vendor, timeframe matters.* If you ignore timing, account executives will be screaming their heads off when all those "hot opportunities" your team passes turn out to be under contract for the next two years.

If your market is mature, I recommend using PACT[2]: pain, authority, consequence, target profile, and *timing*. That addition should prevent your reps from handing over opportunities that are qualified but unable to buy for three or four quarters.

CHAPTER 4

BUILD A SOLID FOUNDATION

BRETT GARRETT, an investor at Rocketship Capital, shared this story about a high-growth company in his portfolio. As with many startups, account executives at this particular company were wearing many hats. They were identifying accounts, reaching out to secure first conversations, conducting discovery calls, working existing opportunities, the works. This created a problem. The reps were so focused on the top of the funnel, on opportunity creation, that they were actually elongating their own sales cycles.

To meet its aggressive growth targets, the company decided to build an in-house sales development team. This not only allowed account executives to focus exclusively on moving prospects through the sales process but also gave the company access to a pool of new candidates to nurture and grow—a farm team for future account executives. "Now, the AEs get to focus on what they're best at, which is selling," shared Brett. "And we can bring in this less experienced talent—that aren't ready to be full-blown closing reps—but who are hungry and eager to learn. It's a huge win-win."

Do Brett's experiences resonate with you? I suspect they do. Before you rush to build out your team, there are three considerations to take into account. The strategy element of sales development goes beyond just *why* and *how*. The factors that support *when* to build must be in place before launching a team. These include the following:

1. **ALIGNMENT:** Are senior leadership, sales, and marketing willing

25

to make the investment in time, energy, and money that will be required to make this kind of team successful? The first rule of sales development is *no fighting in front of the kids*. Shared goals, objectives, and expectations across the management team are a critical component of your success. Every cycle wasted in inter-departmental bickering is a cycle lost to improving execution.

2. **MARKET-MESSAGE FIT:** Do you know enough about your market to build a solid process and messaging that fledgling reps can use to establish credibility over the phone? It takes more than "hungry" to be successful in sales development. Don't make the mistake of thinking that just because you hire eager and aggressive reps that they will be effective. Your prospects don't have time to educate your reps on their businesses. Make sure your onboarding and training leave reps fluent in your prospects' language, thinking, professional goals, etc.

3. **SKILL OF CLOSERS:** Does your sales organization have the attitude and aptitude to take early-stage opportunities and successfully launch the sales process? Take a dispassionate look at your sales team. Are they truly closers, or are they relationship builders? If you're going to invest in building an early-stage team that aggressively focuses on building new pipeline, you need to have account executives who can effectively launch the sales process.

If you answered *yes* to all three, you're ready. Awesome! Now you have to make your next big decision: Where should this team report?

The SDR Wishbone

Early on, the decision needs to be made whether the team should sit within sales or marketing. The sales development group is often the wishbone that gets tugged between the two. I recently published research on the practices of more than 340 business-to-business (B2B) companies with sales development groups. This *SDR Metrics Report* can be found at http://sdrbook.io/SDRMETRICS. I found that the vast majority of companies place sales development under the sales umbrella (76 percent of respondents). One point worth mentioning is that those groups focused *exclusively on inbound lead qualification* were more likely to roll up into marketing. Here is my take:

> *Stop thinking about sales versus marketing. Your team should report to whoever has the bandwidth, expertise, and passion to lead it. Success hinges on who leads the group, not where it sits in the org chart.*

A director of marketing with a track record of building process, recruiting talent, and developing all-stars is far better than an SVP of sales who expects the group to run itself. This is more important than what my (or any other!) research says that "everyone else" is doing.

Expectation Setting

Last year at Dreamforce, Salesforce's gigantic tech conference in San Francisco, I met the VP of sales of a technology services company. She wanted to get my take on the results of her fledgling sales development effort.

Over the previous twelve months, she had launched a team and grown it to four outbound reps. "All in, I think I have spent about $600K on the group so far. We have good forward-looking pipeline. But to date, the group has only sourced $750K in net new business," she shared. She then inquired what I thought of the return.

I replied, "You said your sales cycle is roughly 120 days. I bet you've closed the majority of that revenue in the last four to six months. Am I right?" She said I was. I continued, "And for the six months prior, how much business did your account executives source from net new customers?" She thought for half a beat, smiled, and replied, "Well, about half that, and they cost me a hell of a lot more." We agreed the group was off to a good start and in six months the return would be rock solid.

Setting expectations as you build and grow sales development is critical. Communicating up to the executive level, across to peers, and down to team members takes forethought and planning. Not every sales leader is willing to take the long view, like the one we met above, and consider "compared to what?"

It has been my experience that many executives view sales development as a sort of chemical reaction: *hire a team, add one part CRM to two parts leads and list, and POOF! Instant revenue.* Sadly, it's not quite that simple.

It's a big investment to have a sales development team, an investment of both time and money. Of course, the end game is to get to repeatable pipeline and revenue growth as quickly as possible. But if you have a complex solution or one that requires that your account executives educate the market, you have to think long term.

Devon McDonald knows this well. She is a Partner with OpenView Venture Partners, sits on the firm's investment committee, and oversees its growth team. "For groups setting introductory meetings, business likely won't close for months (or even quarters). That doesn't mean reps don't add immense value along the way," shared Devon. "As you wait for all that pipeline to reach the forecast, consider this team to be a built-in research unit."

Although revenue is the yardstick with which we all love to measure, collecting market intelligence has real value.

Your reps will have more prospect conversations in a week than just about anyone else in the organization: VP of sales, top account executive, and CEO included.

The key is gathering information from each and every interaction and analyzing it to make the organization as a whole smarter. As your reps ramp, they should be building prospect profiles, adding information about status quo solutions, testing messaging, and collecting a dozen other data points. Use that data to formulate a more succinct and powerful go-to-market story.

Make sure your team members know that they're contributing from the get-go. They have a tough job and suffer massive rejection every day. Reward them for collecting relevant information, and celebrate the small wins as the group scales.

I find that too many organizations aren't realistic in setting expectations.

They don't take into account the time it takes to ramp a team or properly account for the length of their sales cycle. They want results now.

A good sales development team adds value from day one. It is up to you to understand the value of the conversations they're having, to quantify that pre-pipeline value, and to communicate it across your organization. *What did they cost?* And *What did they yield?* are important questions. But they are not the end-all for fledgling groups. Sales development is an investment, not a cost center. Embrace that fact, and you are well on your way to setting realistic expectations.

PART 2

SPECIALIZATION

Always be a first rate version of yourself and not a second rate
version of someone else.
JUDY GARLAND

Committing to sales development is the first step. Next, you
need to customize your implementation based on your market
and prospect personas.

In this section, I'll cover:
- ▶ Sourcing inbound, outbound, and allbound pipeline
- ▶ Segmenting your prospect universe
- ▶ Strategies and considerations for role specialization

CHAPTER 5

GO ALLBOUND FOR PIPELINE

IN PART 1, we worked our way through why to build a team. We discussed qualification criteria, covered where the team should report, and wrapped up the nuances for setting expectations properly. These are the fundamentals of sales development strategy. Congratulations, you've just earned your *bachelor of SDR*. (You earned an *associate's* degree for not thinking, "We'll just have our account executives do their own prospecting.")

The next element for accelerating revenue growth with sales development is *specialization*. In my view, these are the good-to-great decisions, and you can't earn your *master of SDR* without them. Now, you may be just beginning your sales development journey. When you first build a group, specialization seems a problem for another day. But I promise you, when you're successful (and you will be), the need to specialize roles arises faster than you might think. Specialization involves addressing two big questions:

1. How should my team tackle our market? (segmenting the prospect universe)

2. How should my group be structured? (role specialization)

Segmenting your prospect universe is about aligning effort with opportunity. In chapter 6, we'll cover building an ideal customer profile and how that affects your group's focus. Role specialization involves separating *inbound SDRs* (lead qualification) and *outbound SDRs* (outbound prospecting) into distinct roles. We'll cover that topic in more detail in chapters 7 and 8. But first, I want to address a big controversy in the sales and marketing industry: *inbound versus outbound.*

The Debate

You can hardly step foot into a discussion of sales development without running into an ever-present (and often overheated) debate. *What is the best way to gain new customers: inbound or outbound?* For our purposes, let's define each category as follows:

- ▶ **INBOUND:** Prospects who take action in response to marketing activity (filling out a web form, signing-up for a trial, attending a webinar, etc.)

- ▶ **OUTBOUND:** Prospects whom your reps target with proactive outreach

The most extreme inbound advocates argue that "interrupting buyers doesn't work anymore!" while strident outbound proponents counter that "sitting and waiting for someone to raise their hand is for the reactive and timid!" These debates can devolve and end in shouts of "Outdated! Barbarian!" and retorts of "Kool-Aid drinker! Coward!" These two camps are passionate about their stances and unwilling to give an inch. Think Hatfield versus McCoy, Sparta versus Troy, or Kanye versus the world.

Here's my take: These debates are an interesting thought exercise at best. At worst, they're irrelevant distractions. Growing your business by converting inbound leads is a wonderful thing. The reality is that the majority of companies source less than half of their pipeline from marketing. Only the tiniest fraction—about 10 percent of companies—are able to source more than three-quarters of pipeline from inbound.

The data in figure 5.1 are from my *Inside Sales Metrics and Compensation* research. You can download a copy at http://sdrbook.io/ISMETRICS.

COMPANY REVENUE	PERCENT MARKETING-SOURCED PIPELINE
< $10M	41%
$10–50M	43%
$50–100M	48%
$100–250M	32%
$250M+	29%

Figure 5.1 – Marketing-sourced pipeline by company revenue

So what does this tell us? To me, it makes the case that even if you're lucky enough to have fantastic marketing, inbound leads still leave a fair bit of pipeline to be found via other means. Outbound calling should be one of them.

The best way I can put it is that the "cold calling is dead" camp is half right. In reality, it's the cold that's dead, not the calling.

More often than not, people use the term "cold calling" when they want to position alternative selling strategies that (totally by coincidence!) utilize their products or services. My point is that no one should be "cold" calling any-more—meaning having only a name and number, but lacking a compelling reason to call. (I'll discuss intelligent outbound prospecting in more detail in part 5.)

It's Allbound

I first heard the term *allbound* from Dan McDade, president and CEO of PointClear, and it is a perfect descriptor. Your philosophy should be inbound + outbound = allbound. Let's leave *inbound versus outbound* to those peddling wares to their respective markets. For the rest of us, we're building sales development to drive opportunities to the top of the funnel. The funnel is entirely agnostic about how opportunities are sourced. Quite frankly, I've never met an account executive who refused an SDR-sourced opportunity on "philosophical grounds."

Ken Krogue is president and co-founder of InsideSales.com. His company is a powerhouse in the sales acceleration space backed by the likes of Kleiner Perkins Caufield & Byers, Salesforce Ventures, and US Venture Partners. From his measurement at Insidesales.com, Ken shared that an inbound opportunity is roughly twice as valuable as one generated through outbound effort. But the challenge—and it's a big one—is that there are exponentially more small companies than big ones. As a result, the vast majority of inbound leads are small.

"If you want to go upmarket, which you absolutely must if you want to grow, you have to go outbound," shared Ken. "Since inbound is worth twice as much as outbound, I say go after accounts twice as big when you go out-bound. Winning large customers is much more about causing a sale, not just catching one."

This is an important point. Rather than say *Inbound leads close faster, so we'll just wait for the big deals to come to us*, Ken and his team have decided to go *allbound*. That doesn't mean calling each and every prospect under the sun. It means identifying the accounts that are the *most* profitable and targeting them with outbound activity. You can accomplish this only if you've segmented your potential prospect universe and built an ideal customer profile. That's exactly what we'll cover in the next chapter.

CHAPTER 6

SELL TO EVERYONE; CLOSE NO ONE

IT WAS 9 A.M. on a Tuesday in April. I was presenting to the CEO, SVP of sales, and VP of marketing for a technology company in their Toronto, Ontario headquarters. Their team had had a string of bad months, and they had brought in my team and me to assess their go-to-market strategy.

I began the executive overview of our findings by sharing, "I've got good news and bad news. The good news is that everyone we spoke with was able to share your company's ideal customer profile (ICP). The bad news is we didn't hear much overlap in their responses." Sadly, this is an all-too-common refrain. Most companies *believe* they have a solid understanding of their ideal customer profile and that it has been communicated across the organization. In reality, they have dozens of different assumptions floating around.

Try this exercise. Ask a senior sales leader to define the characteristics of your ideal prospect. Next, ask a recently hired account executive. Finally, ask your most junior marketing person in charge of demand generation. If those three responses overlap by even 50 percent, count yourself lucky.

For more years than I care to remember, thought leaders and pundits have been banging on about the importance of a shared concept of an ICP. Frankly, we are doing no better today than we were five or even ten years ago. Having your organization in agreement regarding your ICP is a critical success factor. Otherwise, marketing is off generating demand with one prospect profile while sales is expecting leads from another entirely. That is a shotgun approach when today's selling climate requires a sniper rifle. In this chapter, I address that very issue. To help my clients gain clarity, I developed a framework I call *The ABCDs.*

THE ABCDs

Think about your potential prospect universe. Obviously, some prospects are more ideal than others. The rub lies in the nebulous nature of the word *ideal.* Take a piece of paper and draw a 2×4 table similar to figure 6.1:

Figure 6.1 –ABCDs starting point

Now, jot down some common characteristics of each tier of your prospect universe. Here's how you might begin to categorize your market.

▶ **A: A-LIST.** These are your dream clients, the ones you absolutely want to do business with. They can make your quarter and change the direction of your company. They have a problem, you have the solution, you know it, and they'll figure it out (sooner or later). Some companies call these named or strategic accounts.

▶ **B: BREAD & BUTTER.** This is your sweet spot. These types of accounts—hopefully there are thousands of them—should all be doing business with you. There are too many to list by name, but you can easily define a few key traits they share (e.g., five hundred to four thousand employees, five remote offices, running Google Apps for Business).

▶ **C: COMPELLING EVENTS.** These are accounts that generally don't have a pressing need for your solution, but then . . . BAM! An internal or external shock shakes up their priorities. This could be an acquisition, a bad quarter, or a change in leadership.

▶ **D: DEAD ENDS.** These accounts may want to work with you. They may even *need* to buy from you, but for whatever reason they can't or won't. The biggest problems with Dead End accounts are that they look and sound just like Bread & Butters. The key is identifying red flags and preventing your reps from wasting time here.

Filling in your boxes might leave you with something like figure 6.2:

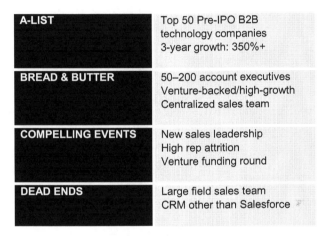

A-LIST	Top 50 Pre-IPO B2B technology companies 3-year growth: 350%+
BREAD & BUTTER	50–200 account executives Venture-backed/high-growth Centralized sales team
COMPELLING EVENTS	New sales leadership High rep attrition Venture funding round
DEAD ENDS	Large field sales team CRM other than Salesforce

Figure 6.2 – Filled in ABCDs

Account Prioritization

Whether your strategy involves inbound, outbound, or allbound, prioritizing your prospect base is a must. Once you've built your account prioritization, it's time to think about aligning effort to opportunity. Here are a few considerations:

▶ **A-LIST:** These accounts rarely come inbound. That's the nature of whale hunting—they stubbornly refuse to harpoon themselves. This is where you want reps to spend a high percentage of their outbound cycles. Because these accounts will have numerous people and functional areas for you to target, expect your reps to have at least one target title at play in their process at any given moment.

▶ **BREAD & BUTTER:** Here's where your inbound SDRs will typically spend the bulk of their time. Ideally, these are the types of prospects responding to marketing campaigns. Outbound SDRs should focus on the sub-markets, verticals, and traits that are correlated with the highest-probability (and profitability) accounts. Remember Ken Krogue's advice? *If inbound is twice as valuable, go after accounts twice as large with outbound.* Use outbound to target only the largest of your Bread &Butter accounts.

▶ **COMPELLING EVENTS:** When prospects have pain and come inbound, it's a wonderful thing. The single best compelling event in all of sales is "because the government said I had to do so." But be warned, compelling events can be hit or miss for outbound efforts. The same trigger events that you'll have identified are likely to be spotted by your competitors too. Ask any VP of sales after their company takes a venture capital funding round. It feels like open season and they're the deer.

▶ **DEAD ENDS:** There isn't much you can do to prevent these accounts from showing up with inbound. Your reps need to sniff them out and professionally disengage. Prospecting and passing a Dead End account only to have it rejected by an account executive is a lesson just about every sales development rep has to learn.

Let's pause for a status check. We know we want SDR-sourced opportunities from both inbound and outbound. We've also identified which types of accounts have the highest return on effort. One question remains: *can a single rep be tasked with both inbound qualification and outbound prospecting?* In the next few chapters, we'll discuss the ins and outs of role specialization and if/when you should create multiple sales development roles.

CHAPTER 7

SPECIALIZE TO ACCELERATE

A BRIEF (but totally incomplete) history of specialization:

Agricultural: last ten thousand years
Industrial: last hundred and thirty years
Prospectors/Closers: last forty years
Inbound/Outbound SDRs: last fifteen years

In the history of business-to-business selling, sales development is a relatively recent development. Role specialization—the practice of breaking *inbound SDRs* (lead qualification) and *outbound SDRs* (outbound prospecting) into separate roles—is still in its infancy. And yet, this approach has quickly taken root as it delivers big returns.

Think back to the two companies we met in chapter 1. Acquia decided to specialize into *inbound qualifiers* and *outbound prospectors*. Listrak built a *data gathering* team separate from the *introductory meeting setting* group. From my research, I know that roughly 50 percent of technology companies (a group quick to adopt new techniques) have implemented role specialization. That's more than double the proportion doing so just three years ago.

This trend is here to stay. CA Technologies understands this. Sid Kumar, its vice president of global inside sales, shared, "Having the right model for the right situation is key. Customers don't care about your coverage model—they only want to understand how you meet their business objectives. The right coverage model, aligned to your strategy, maximizes your chances of turning prospects into customers."

Sales development specialization is an accelerator on the path to repeatable and scalable pipeline. I believe in its power. But I also know that not every company can (or should) specialize its teams. Your ability to do so hinges on a number of factors. Let me share some thoughts to support you along the way.

The Logic of Specialization

Before you commit, you'll need to agree with the "whys" of SDR specialization. As I see it, there are three main reasons: *focus, attitude and aptitude*, and *human nature*.

- ▶ **FOCUS:** You want your reps to have appropriate processes and tools to ensure they are successful. It is easier to measure and optimize execution for a specialist than for a jack-of-all-trades. Once your team reaches a certain size, say more than four reps, you can start to consider specialization.

- ▶ **ATTITUDE AND APTITUDE:** Not every rep who excels at one area is well suited for the other. Although the outcomes are the same—introductory meetings or qualified opportunities—reps who thrive on cultivating inbound leads aren't always built for hunting the big game of outbound.

- ▶ **HUMAN NATURE:** When you have reps in a blended role, they'll inevitably spend more time where they're most comfortable. In the vast majority of cases, that means focusing on inbound leads. Reps will chase bad inbound leads rather than invest the time in outbound prospecting into *A-List* accounts. We all tend to take the path of least resistance. *Checking in* or *following up* with low-probability inbound leads is much easier than going outbound to a cold, though ideal, prospect.

I've identified half a dozen factors in which the roles differ. Figure 7.1 lays them out for you.

The Decisive Half-Dozen

	INBOUND ROLE	OUTBOUND ROLE
EXPERIENCE	Limited to no sales experience	Previous experience (aren't phone allergic)
ATTITUDE	Able to juggle inbound "flow"—handles interruptions	Able to handle rejection—resilient individual
LEVEL OF PROSPECT	Comfortable working with influencer/user level	Comfortable targeting senior decision makers
LEVEL OF INTEREST	Prospects already grasp portion of value proposition	Prospects don't yet recognize a need or pain
MESSAGING	"How can I help you?" and guide to next step	"Reframe your thinking" and challenge the status quo
TIME TO RAMP	Quicker: well-defined process and high quantity of prospect interactions	Slower: takes time to master business-centric conversations

Figure 7.1 – Six factors where inbound and outbound skill sets differ

If you've embraced the *why* behind specialization, now you have to put together a plan of attack. The next few sections will help you do just that.

Inbound Team Structure

When sales development first emerged, reps were typically partnered with three or four account executives. If sales had geographic territories, so did the sales development team. It made for a nice, tidy package that didn't require a lot of thought. While this still sometimes works for outbound SDRs, it rarely does for inbound SDRs.

The reason: *setting equitable inbound quotas is a nightmare.* No matter how hard you try, your inbound leads stubbornly refuse to arrive in equal shares per territory. (*How rude!*) That leaves you with uneven lead flow. Here's an example of the problems this can cause. Let's assume the following:

▶ You have three major territories: East, Central, West.

▶ Each inbound rep has the same quota.

▶ The vast majority of your leads are from technology companies— which are heavily weighted East and West.

▶ Your central territory gets 40 percent less lead volume.

In this scenario, your East and West reps are killing their number while the Central rep is struggling. Now, the Central account executives are blaming the poor SDR for not passing enough leads. You get where I'm going. Geographic territories are great on paper but a nightmare when assigned to inbound teams.

To address this issue, I recommend one of two approaches: territory-based (customized quotas) or round robin (uniform quotas).Option #1, territory-based quotas, is for those who enjoy filing tax returns. *Do you love math? Is Excel on a Sunday morning your own personal nirvana?* If you answered *yes* to both, then have I got the thing for you! This approach requires you to predict future lead flow per territory. You will then estimate conversion rates and set a unique quota per territory. In this scenario, the reps receive fair, territory-specific quotas, and you gain 20 percent more gray hair.

Option #2, round-robin, is much easier. In this model, leads are distributed to inbound SDRs in turn. You don't have to break out the abacus to assign customized quotas, and each rep has an equal opportunity to make his or her number. Nice and tidy. Because SDRs won't consistently work with the same account executives, the round robin approach doesn't allow for the tight bond—and informal mentoring—between team members. Nonetheless, I believe the benefits outweigh the costs.

You should strongly consider this approach as long as you can automate the lead distribution process. You don't want to have *a person* responsible for manually distributing leads. Number one, they'll quickly become the clog in the funnel. Number two, you'll probably get stuck with the task. Number three, it will lead to charges of favoritism. *Why are you giving Kyle all the good leads?* Removing bias, real or imagined, is a major benefit of round robin territories.

To help you think through headcount, let me share some capacity guidelines. One inbound SDR can typically handle about two hundred to three hundred leads a month when fully ramped. There is some variation based on average selling price, data quality, and other factors. But in my experience, this seems to be the magic number.

Outbound Team Structure

Three approaches are most common for structuring outbound sales development teams:

1. Partnering outbound SDRs with specific account executives

2. Assigning outbound SDRs *named* or *strategic* accounts

3. A blend of both (specific account executives and specific accounts)

You can be successful with any of the three—assuming that the account executive territories have been properly built and balanced. Just remember: outbound efforts need to be extremely focused. You don't want your outbound SDRs investing time chasing just anyone. Outbound strategies require a tightly defined list of who is worth calling. As we discussed in chapter 6, this includes your A-List and Bread & Butter accounts.

One outbound SDR can typically target one hundred to two hundred accounts per month. This is cumulative, not net new. During the month, some accounts will be qualified and others disqualified, and the rest will remain in a working status. At this point, you might be wondering about setting quotas. Hold that thought, as we'll cover quotas later on.

Rules of Engagement

There's one more consideration I'd like to cover: *channel conflict*. You need to create rules of engagement to address potential collisions between inbound and outbound teams. Imagine the following scenario:

▶ An outbound SDR targets Steve Winter, EVP, worldwide sales and operations for Marketo.

▶ Steve doesn't return the calls and emails.

▶ Ten days after the final email, Bill Binch, Marketo's SVP of global SMB sales, becomes an inbound lead.

▶ Who gets to work that lead?

Or imagine the reverse. Can an inbound lead that was never qualified be targeted by your outbound team? After how long of a cooling-off period? You need rules to handle instances like these. Don't underestimate the amount of bad blood these situations can cause (not to mention the hours you'll lose to arbitrating inbound/outbound disputes).

Sadly, there is no *perfect* length of time that works for each and every company. Much will depend on your sales cycle and the size of your target account. For example, in a relatively simple, high-volume sales process, thirty days after last touch could be your holding period. For an enterprise sale, you might need a much longer timeframe.

No one rule will satisfy every rep in every scenario. *That's a guarantee!* You'll have to mediate disputes as they arise. But if you consistently apply a single policy, it should (more or less) even out over time.

CHAPTER 8

CONSIDER THE RESEARCH ROLE

IF YOUR AVERAGE SELLING PRICE is sufficiently high or you are in a land grab situation, I'm advocating that you consider adding another sales development role: "lead researcher."

So far, we've discussed:
Prospecting versus closing?   *Check.*
Inbound versus outbound?   *Check.*

But what about:
Data gathering versus dialing?   *Che . . . wait. What?*

The lead researcher role is all about streamlining the pre-calling process. It affects productivity in two ways. One, it enables sales access. If your reps have the correct titles, email address, and direct-dial phone numbers (the true holy grail of prospecting), they'll have more conversations. This has been demonstrated time and again. Two, it enables context.

Researching individual prospects and identifying customized research points takes time. Sadly, there's no automatic "Perfect Message Generator." If your reps have compelling events and key research points at their fingertips, they will have better conversations. Access and context are the primary reasons to consider the lead researcher role.

Access

The most widely applicable use case for this role is around data hygiene. Exact titles, org charts, email addresses, and direct-dial phone numbers are major productivity boosters. Earlier, we met Ross Kramer and his company, Listrak. If you recall, Listrak built a separate *data gathering* team to support the outbound SDRs. As Ross shared, "Noodling on your data inside of CRM is a great way to avoid making calls. That's why we do a separation of church and state. The people making the calls don't update the data."

Candidly, Ross is a numbers guy. He's done the math and knows that his outbound reps need to be on the phone—not scouring LinkedIn, Data.com, InsideView, and other tools, fabulous though they might be.

Context

I remember working with one client who sold large-ticket services to publicly traded companies. The company's sales cycles were long and highly complex. When I met the company's chief revenue officer, she said they were seeking to boost the productivity of their outbound team.

Taking a look at where the reps were spending their time, I found something interesting. Nearly one-fifth of rep time was spent reviewing target account quarterly earnings calls for "nuggets" to use in their prospecting. These sales triggers made for highly effective sales messaging, but they took significant time to uncover. Two things jumped out at me. They're probably standing out for you, too.

1. **WHY THE SDRS?** Is the type of person who is great at finding sales triggers in quarterly earnings calls the same type of person who excels at aggressively prospecting on the phone? Probably not.

2. **WHAT'S THE OPPORTUNITY COST?** We know that jumping back and forth between activities increases errors and lengthens the time to completion. Now imagine if your reps were scanning earnings calls as part of routine pre-call planning. Sounds like a recipe for low activity volume (at best) and serious call avoidance (at worst).

With this client, I recommended introducing a *pre-sales analyst* role. These reps' sole function was to comb through earnings calls and summarize relevant tidbits. They then produced "talking points" memos and attached them to accounts in Salesforce. When the SDRs went to conduct their pre-call planning, they had all this fantastic research at their fingertips. Their job was to take that data and leverage it in their messaging.

And it worked—big time. A few months after integrating the analyst role, scheduled meetings jumped 20 percent. The chief revenue officer shared that hiring new SDRs had also become much easier. "We stopped looking for finance majors who wanted to break into sales," she shared. "Now we're able to focus on smart and driven candidates from all backgrounds. That's a much larger pool to draw from."

Again, adding this role isn't for everyone. But I hope you take the spirit of this chapter to heart. Perhaps you don't need a team of reps to deliver access and context data. Perhaps you can purchase a technology to do the enablement work for you.

Let me end with this: if you can invest $1 in improving processes or improving data, I'd choose data all day every day. A good rep with great processes and okay data will struggle. It's like sprinting on a muddy field. A good rep with okay processes and great data is off to the races, running with a strong wind at his or her back. Clearly, not every company has the need for lead researchers. You should consider adding the role if two or more of the following ring true:

▶ You have a dedicated outbound SDR team.

▶ Your reps are juggling multiple tools to build account and contact lists.

▶ The profiling data that separate an A-List account from a Dead End isn't easy (or cost effective) to lay hands on.

▶ Your reps are spending significant time identifying relevant research points.
Your reps are calling into popular titles and need deep research to stand out. (*Hello, VP of sales and CIO!*)

Outsourced lead generation/appointment setting firms were the first to embrace this role. They are our early adopters. In my experience, they understand the economics of the sales development role better than just about anyone. They've done the math on what one extra direct dial, one fewer bounced email, and one more research point mean to the bottom line.

CHAPTER 9

FOLLOW THE EARLY ADOPTERS

I WANT TO END PART 2 by sharing stories of how two sales development leaders implemented specialization. Up to this point, I've given you a clear picture of the *whys* and *hows*. Now, I want to share how it all comes together.

Casey Corrigan is a leader who knows how to build and scale sales development teams. Currently, he is director of sales at Lytics. During his time at Good Data, he made the decision to separate inbound and outbound into distinct roles. "We split the role for three reasons. First, lead routing rules had become complicated to the point of being cumbersome. Second, reps were constantly shifting gears between inbound and outbound. That was impacting momentum. Finally, reps followed the money as the compensation plan paid at different rates for inbound versus outbound."

To address these issues, Casey built two groups as follows:

- ► **THE INBOUND TEAM:** Leads were distributed on a first-come, first-serve basis to whichever reps were available. The priority was on speed of engagement. Inbound SDRs were charged with doing a deep level of qualification and generating qualified opportunities.

- ► **THE OUTBOUND TEAM:** Territories were divided by geography and product. Initially, reps were measured on the number of introductory meetings—a less strict qualification criterion than their inbound counterparts. Over time, as the outbound effort matured, the model migrated to generating qualified opportunities.

The approach isn't without its challenges. Due to the round robin of leads, the reps on the inbound won't develop the deep personal relationships with the account execs that the teamed outbound reps enjoy. Also, staffing the inbound team perfectly is a challenge due to natural peaks and valleys in lead volume. Nevertheless, Casey shared that after adopting the round robin approach, productivity had increased by nearly 30 percent.

Here's another example. Carlos Garcia, sales development manager at Smart Bear, previously led the prospecting team at Ping Identity. While there, he built an inbound team to work marketing leads and an outbound group to fill in the gaps. Carlos structured the teams as follows:

▶ **THE INBOUND TEAM:** Leads were assigned round robin with a goal of reaching every lead in less than one business day. A downside of this commitment is that reps were often "shackled to what comes in"—as they lacked any control over the next name on their prospecting list.

▶ **THE OUTBOUND TEAM:** This group focused on target accounts. They deeply qualified opportunities before passing to sales counterparts. Without the (often distracting) flow of inbound leads, reps were more strategic about planning their days.

A few points of commonality jump out at me from Carlos's and Casey's experiences. One, if speed to contact is your goal, you need a specialized inbound team. Territories, routing, process, and handoff all need to be oriented toward immediate follow-up. Two, it is difficult to balance meeting SLA commitments with marketing while also giving reps the latitude to decide who/who not to call. This is an important distinction and one we'll discuss more deeply later on.

PART 3

RECRUITING

Every successful sales development effort is backed by outstanding people. Now it's time to find yours.

In this section, I'll cover:
- ▶ Innovating to out-recruit the competition
- ▶ Creating a hiring process that rocks
- ▶ Tools and strategies to scale hiring

CHAPTER 10

HIRE WITH URGENCY

DURING THE GREAT RECESSION (February 2008 to February 2010), filling an open sales development seat was easy. Hiring managers were flooded with applications from both green and experienced candidates. Those days were the epitome of a buyer's market (meaning the companies doing the hiring were in control).

Those days are gone.

Today, the quantity of open positions far outstrips the supply of qualified candidates actively searching for SDR roles. Three trends are converging to make this role the epicenter of a major talent competition.

1. **DEMAND:** Second to perhaps only top-shelf sales engineers, there is no hotter commodity in individual contributor recruitment. I recently ran a LinkedIn Job search and found just more than 3,400 postings for sales development. After quickly skimming through several dozen job descriptions, I can tell you they all sound *exactly* the same (I'll discuss more on fixing that in chapter 12).

2. **SUPPLY:** Believe it or not, not every rep wants to remain an SDR until retirement. The vast majority are using the role as their entry into the professional world. They rightly think, "If I can make it here, I can make it anywhere." The flow of new candidates hasn't done much to increase the amount of available talent. Fully two-thirds of

first-time SDRs are being promoted up or otherwise moving out of the role within eighteen months.

3. **CALIBER:** The vast majority of companies are looking for *six or more months of sales/sales-adjacent experience*. In the words of renowned American philosopher Mike Tyson, "Everybody has a plan until they get punched in the mouth." There is a world of difference between a candidate who thinks he or she can succeed on the phones (has a plan) and one who has survived two full quarters of living the job (has been punched in the mouth).

The only way to stay in front of this reality is to out-hire your competitors. Not coincidentally, the third element for accelerating revenue growth with sales development is *recruiting*. In this part of the book, I'll argue that the focus on recruiting needs to be upgraded from *important* to *urgent*. I'll share the attributes of ideal candidates, ways to attract top talent, and a hiring process that can't be beat. By implementing these strategies, you'll take your recruiting to the next level and beat every other company that's hiring in the competition for talent.

The Time Crunch

If you're like most executives, your calendar is already full. You have more on your plate than any mere mortal could be expected to handle. Whether you're building a group from scratch, expanding the team, or just trying to backfill an open position, recruiting tends to slip into the *important, but not urgent* bucket.

> *Every leader intends to make time for hiring. But time for recruiting won't ever be found—it has to be made. Your calendar eats your intentions for breakfast. Period.*

You, and/or your first-line leaders, need to make recruiting a top three priority. I guarantee you, if you don't start out with this mindset, recruiting will slip further and further down your list. Tell me if this sounds familiar: It's 7 a.m. on Monday. Traffic was unbelievably light, and you got a prime parking spot. Life is good, and you're ready to rock. Here's where you start the week (figure 10.1):

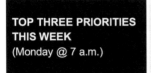

TOP THREE PRIORITIES THIS WEEK (Monday @ 7 a.m.)	1.	Source A-player candidates
	2.	One-on-one coaching sessions
	3.	Plan for next month and next quarter

Figure 10.1 – Monday morning's ambition

By 10 a.m., you already start to feel your plan slipping a bit, because the new technology implementation has hit a snag. And by Tuesday afternoon, the plan seems like a distant memory. Excellent, the CFO wants to talk about the compensation plan again. Wednesday, Thursday, and Friday are a blur of minor emergencies, meetings, reporting, and sundry whack-a-mole tasks. Here's where you end the week (figure 10.2):

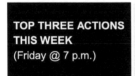

TOP THREE ACTIONS THIS WEEK (Friday @ 7 p.m.)	1.	Running reports for my boss/board
	2.	Putting out fires
	3.	"Got a minute" questions from reps

Figure 10.2 – Friday afternoon's reality

Mark Roberge has lived this reality. At the time of this writing, he is the chief revenue officer of HubSpot Sales Products. From 2007 to 2013, Mark served as HubSpot's SVP of worldwide sales and services. During that time, he expanded the sales group from a handful of reps to more than 450 people. "When I was in the early stages of building the team, and we had essentially a dozen reps in a garage, I had to hire roughly one rep a month. I had no resources—no recruiting team, no training team, no first-line managers, no one but me. I knew if I tried to do all those things well, it would literally add up to a 150-hour work week."

Rather than going a mile wide and an inch deep in all those areas, Mark decided he would elevate recruiting and make it his prime focus. "I came to the conclusion that hiring had to be my number one priority," commented Mark. "I felt that if I could get the right people into the system, even if I did a mediocre job at training and management, they would find a way to win. But if I got mediocre people in, even if I did a world-class job at training and leading, it wouldn't matter."

Have I convinced you to make hiring a top three priority? I hope I have. Staying focused on the future requires discipline. In the remainder of this chapter, I'm going to lay out a strategy for making the job a bit easier.

Hiring in Groups

It is a truth universally acknowledged that a manager in possession of unfilled headcount must be in want of his or her sanity. Said more plainly, filling open positions is enough to make you lose your mind.

If you want any time whatsoever to focus on things other than recruitment—or, as your boss might call those tasks, "your real job"—you'll want to embrace hiring in groups. The massive efficiency gains from hiring two or more reps simultaneously vastly outweigh the boldness of the proposition. Here are three big benefits:

1. **ONBOARDING IS SIMPLIFIED:** Think about the people whose time and attention you will need to effectively ramp your new reps (product, marketing, sales enablement, etc.). Training for one single rep tends to be informal, ad hoc, and (too often) sloppy, but training a "class" demands more attention and quality preparation.

2. **YOUR TIME IS PROTECTED:** Ramping a new hire is a significant time commitment for an SDR leader. Running one new hire through onboarding = *1 unit* of effort. Running three new hires (one at a time) = *3 units*. Running three new hires (as a group) = only slightly more than *1 unit*. The efficiency gains are too massive to ignore.

3. **NEW HIRES BOND TOGETHER:** A *class mentality* leads to peer-to-peer coaching, better brainstorming, and a healthy competitive spirit. New hires are able to share what they're learning, ask each other questions, and have an apples-to-apples benchmark for their results.

Natasha Sekkat is VP sales development for VMTurbo. She previously served as global director, inside sales centers of excellence at EMC. We discussed hiring in groups, and Natasha shared that the big benefit is that new reps don't feel like they're alone. There's a sense of camaraderie from seeing peers going through the exact same experience. "They begin to learn from each other, too," she shared. "Instead of it being solely on the manager to bring people along and teach them everything, you get this cohort mentality where they're sharing their ideas. Reps will still be learning at slightly different paces, but the people that move forward pull those moving less quickly along with them."

The benefits Natasha outlined are too big to ignore. If you're launching a sales development group from scratch, you absolutely want to hire as a class. I suggest you budget for an initial headcount of at least three reps. Hire fewer reps, and a single rep's departure (voluntary or otherwise) can really set you back.

If your group is new, you'll likely still be refining and iterating your ideal customer profile and messaging. The smaller the group, the more difficult it is to determine if the *market/message* is off or if the *rep/messenger* isn't right for the role. One successful rep is beginner's luck. Two is a coincidence. But three is a trend! When it comes time to scale, you need to know that your process is repeatable and that your message is on point. Whenever possible, plan to hire in groups. You'll learn a ton along the way, and you'll be better prepared for hiring and onboarding your next class of reps.

CHAPTER 11

SPOT QUALITIES OF QUALIFIED CANDIDATES

DAVID OGILVY has one heck of a life story.

Considered by many to be the father of advertising, Ogilvy immigrated to the United States from England and joined the Audience Research Institute (the precursor of Gallup) in the 1930s. During the Second World War, he worked for the British Intelligence Service in Washington, DC. In 1948, he founded the ad agency Hewitt, Ogilvy, Benson & Mather. He was made a Commander of the Order of the British Empire, elected to the Advertising Hall of Fame, and awarded France's Order of Arts and Letters. Not too shabby a run.

He was also unbelievably quotable. One of my favorites of his is about people.

> *"If you always hire people who are smaller than you are, we shall become a company of dwarfs. If, on the other hand, you always hire people who are bigger than you are, we shall become a company of giants."*

Let me say upfront, I don't have a strict type (or stereotype) of "what a great SDR looks like." Quite a number of companies exclusively hire recent college grads, and that works for them. A fair number hire reps with two or more years of professional experience and achieve an equal measure of success. Keep an open mind about the profile you're looking for. Diversity of thought and experience is incredibly valuable.

Bear in mind, you can have the best process, product, and message in the world, but if you hire the wrong people, it is all for naught. Recruiting is made much less challenging if you begin from a solid foundation. It all starts with having a solid candidate profile. This is the gold standard against which you will measure candidates. In the rest of this chapter, I'll share my take on what it means to hire future giants.

At a minimum, you should have the following four candidate profiles in mind: *recent/upcoming university graduates, experienced SDRs, military-to-civilian transitions,* and *job shifters* (those looking to make the move into professional selling). In terms of what you're looking for within those profiles, focus on the following:

There are three characteristics that are universal in the best sales development candidates: passion, competitiveness, and curiosity.

Let's look at these three qualities in more detail and why you want candidates who possess them.

Passion

In sales in general, it is difficult to succeed without passion. In a sales development role in particular, it is next to impossible. Your reps will face a unique blend of monotony and rejection with a light dusting of intermittent triumph. All the cash, leaderboards, and praise in the world can't keep someone striving in this role. It has to come from within.

When I say passion, I mean perseverance and grit over the long term. Dr. Angela Duckworth, a professor at the University of Pennsylvania, has done amazing research on grit and writes that "the gritty individual approaches achievement as a marathon; his or her advantage is stamina." Given the choice between someone who is naturally brilliant and someone who is passionate about sales, I'd choose the latter all day long.

Nick Hedges is CEO and president of Velocify. I asked Nick for his take on hiring, and he shared, "I like to ask candidates to tell me about something they love to do and why. Then I'll ask them why they love the idea of working in sales for me. Most people will unconsciously communicate their passion for something they personally care about. I compare that to how passionate they sound about the position they're applying for."

This is a great way to separate the truly interested from those just looking to land a job. A word to the wise: there can be a big disparity between *how excited a candidate is about getting an offer* and *how excited a new hire is to do the job*. Recently, I was working with the director of a large sales development team. He confessed to me that he budgets a 10 percent "never mind" rate (reps who accepted an offer and retract it before their first day). Such is the reality when hiring recent grads. Screening for passion is one way to mitigate this reality.

Passion plus great leadership equals success. You can train just about anyone on your market, your prospects, and your process. But all the cash, technologies, and training in the world won't light a fire in someone's belly.

Competitiveness

As a leader, your job is to build a great team. Emphasis on the word *team*. You need reps who are competitive but aren't slash-and-burn mercenaries. A successful sales development environment requires balancing the opportunity to compete, the reward for winning, and the learning that comes from competing.

Alison Gooch is a senior sales leader at Pardot, a Salesforce subsidiary. We both happened to be speaking at the Rainmaker conference in Atlanta. I sat in on her session, and she described the attributes of her ideal sales development candidate. Ali shared that she looks for "compassionate competitors—reps who like to win, but not at the expense of their teammates."

I love that descriptor. In reality, the biggest competition for any sales development rep is the prospect's status quo—not the rep in the next cubicle over. Peer coaching, group learning, and celebrating team wins are hallmarks of great teams. Reps who view their knowledge as their personal intellectual property—or someone else's success as their failure—do more harm than good.

Curiosity

You want reps who are intellectually curious lifelong learners and who strive to figure out what works and try new things. If candidates are content with *the way things are,* they aren't going to be successful—being an SDR is part instigator and part detective.

Sales development is more than getting prospects on the phone, asking a series of rapid-fire questions, and documenting their responses. The job is about arousing curiosity and generating interest. Often, that requires getting at the answer behind the answer. Ask your candidates how they prepared for the interview. One might have done some reading on top blogs. Another might have viewed a recorded webinar on your prospects and your industry, while another might have downloaded every piece of content on your website.

Peter Gracey is CEO of prospecting software company QuotaFactory. Pete and I discussed screening for curiosity when hiring. He shared that during interviews he makes sure to give candidates the opportunity to ask about his company, his product, and him personally. "Curious people ask the best questions," shared Pete. "Reps who are genuinely curious have an advantage when prospecting. Questioning is in their DNA; they don't have to fake it."

Sample Interview Questions

Here are some interview questions you might use. These will give you a sense of how to screen for passionate, competitive, and curious individuals.

> **PASSION**
> What's something you're obsessed with right now?
> What gives you a sense of accomplishment?
> What's the hardest task you've recently tackled?

COMPETITIVENESS

Tell me about the last time you were competitive.

Where are you currently competing with friends (e.g., fantasy sports, running, golf)? Where are you in the ranking?

Would you rather be the #1 rep while the team misses the number? Or be #2 while the team hits the goal?

CURIOSITY

When was the last time you had to learn a new skill? How did you go about it?

What is the last book you read?

In prepping for this interview, what surprised you about our company?

Hiring is tough. Not only is it hard to find great candidates, but making sure you hire the best of the best requires patience. Knowing what to look for is a key ingredient of success, but staying true to those requirements takes fortitude. Stay the course, and don't rush to hire.

When I'm faced with a hiring decision, I often think about a quote from VISA founder and former CEO Dee Hock:

"Hire and promote first on the basis of integrity; second, motivation; third, capacity; fourth, understanding; fifth, knowledge; and last and least, experience. Without integrity, motivation is dangerous; without motivation, capacity is impotent; without capacity, understanding is limited; without understanding, knowledge is meaningless; without knowledge, experience is blind. Experience is easy to provide and quickly put to good use by people with all the other qualities."

CHAPTER 12

WRITE JOB DESCRIPTIONS, NOT SLEEP PRESCRIPTIONS

"REPORTING TO THE SALES DEVELOPMENT MANAGER, the corporate SDR is accountable for booking sales demos across all verticals for the closing representative. They will be responsible for proactive calling and lead activity management owning the prospecting stage from . . ." zzzzzzzz.

Sorry. Nodded off there. The above example is how the vast majority of sales development job descriptions sound. In a word: *dreary.* They are about as captivating and inspiring as the operating manual for my toaster.

Most of us were taught that a job description should, well, describe the job. But that's totally backwards.

A job description should sell the job. If you can't capture attention and interest, who the hell cares about the fine print.

For the rest of this chapter, every time you read "job description," think "role elevator pitch." (I've included several examples later on in this chapter to give a feel for what this means.) Your job description should be an amazing piece of content that you'll use to attract the best talent. In a highly competitive market, you'll be selling the sizzle, while every other hiring manager will be documenting the chemical makeup of the steak.

The Sorry State of Job Posts

Our job descriptions should leave candidates with just one impression: *this is the place to advance my career.* Let me tell you just how rare this is. I recently asked a pool of ten up-and-coming SDRs to look at one hundred different job postings. If at least two reps said any one of the jobs looked interesting, I flagged it as a good example.

So how many do you think passed this (admittedly low) bar? Turns out, just about 9 percent. Yup, that's fewer than one in ten. And remember, each post needed to receive only two thumbs up. Just ugly.

I took a look at the 91 percent that didn't make the grade, and what I found shouldn't surprise you. They were buzzwordy, boilerplate, and boring. They did a great job *describing the job* and an absolutely atrocious job *selling it.* There are, however, companies that are doing it right. Let me give you four examples of truly great job descriptions.

Example 1: Zenefits

> Zenefits is the fastest-growing "Software as a Service" (SaaS) company ever. The founders managed to hit on a great idea at just the right time, and now they're reaping the rewards. Two years ago, we had six employees and zero customers. Only a year later, the company had hired 212 employees and signed over 2,000 customers.
>
> A Sales Development Representative is a salesperson-in-training. For a year, you'll help Account Executives cultivate leads and sell Zenefits to businesses.
>
> After a year of apprenticeship, you'll begin to nurture leads of your own, and will take a generous commission for the relationships you help to create . . . which means that if you work hard, you can out-earn many of your peers.

If I were a job seeker, here's how I would see it. First, it makes the founders sound like regular guys who hit on an idea and made it happen. Nothing magic; it can happen to you too. Second, it sets the stage that the SDR role is an apprenticeship. It screams, *you can move up and make big money here.* Hey, compassionate competitor or not, today's SDRs aren't allergic to making the big bucks. Finally, it's written in an authentic, human voice. You get a feel for the culture right from the get-go.

Example 2: Bit9+Carbon Black

> The Sales Development Representative is responsible for identifying and qualifying sales opportunities for Bit9+Carbon Black's sales organization. There is not a high degree of technical knowledge required for this position. This position lays the foundation for a successful high tech sales career. There is a path for career growth within Bit9+Carbon Black for the right candidate that is willing to learn and work toward that goal.
>
> **Your first 3-6 months**
> - Learn the Bit9 products and messaging
> - Learn the tools necessary to be successful: CRM, scripts, WebEx, product info
> - Build relationships with your Inside, Field, and Sales Engineering counterparts
> - Leverage any opportunity you can to learn the market and the business
> - Consistently meet goals for initial presentation setup
>
> **6-18 months**
> - Continue to build on your core skills and product/industry knowledge
> - Know what it takes to meet or exceed your goals and maintain the momentum to do so
> - Begin to expand your knowledge of Inside Sales duties and responsibilities
> - Work with mentors to set goals for yourself to gain consideration for promotion

This example lays out the plan for how to be successful. It isn't a laundry list of job duties, but rather it paints a picture of how the candidate will learn and grow in the position. It does what so few job descriptions do: it answers *why work here* before addressing *what you'll be doing here day to day.* Remember, your descriptions should sell the role, not document the duties.

Example 3: Acquia

Are you looking to jump-start your career with one of the fastest-growing technology companies in America? Are you comfortable being surrounded by incredibly smart and driven people that push you to be better? If you're looking for rapid career growth and are inherently all of these things, read on— you might fit with us!

Acquia's world class sales team is looking to capitalize on the momentum that comes with being the fastest-growing software company in the United States. A big part of that strategy is growing our team of Business Development Representatives.

We're looking for recent college grads that want to jump-start their career through enterprise sales and business development. Did you know that 40 percent of S&P 500 CEOs come from sales & marketing backgrounds? Previous sales experience in technology doesn't hurt, but it isn't a requirement (the majority of our team came directly from the dorm to our office!).

I want you to notice two things about this example. One, they are clearly and directly speaking to recent (and imminent) college grads. They know their target demographic, and they're marketing directly to them. Two, they speak to candidates' aspirations. The line "40 percent of S&P 500 CEOs come from sales & marketing backgrounds" is killer. More often than not, when people graduate from college, they don't run out the door waving their diplomas and hollering, "Give me a list, give me a phone, I'm ready to hammer out some dials!" It is more often a circuitous route that leads them to inside sales. Knowing this, Acquia is communicating, *you need these skills— they'll help shape your future success no matter where you want to end up.* That is powerful stuff.

Example 4: HubSpot

In addition to a standard job description, HubSpot has produced a 70-second job-specific video (http://sdrbook.io/HUBSPOTVIDEO). Here are a few snippets that jumped out at me:

> "We're looking for people who have a desire for sales and are looking to start their career."
>
> "What I think is exciting about the BDR role is that we're a really close-knit group. A few weeks ago, we had a trampoline dodge ball tournament. That was a really fun and great way for the group to get together and feel like a team."
>
> "Aside from all the fun, if you do really well in the BDR role, , the opportunity for growth in the sales organization will definitely be there for you."

There is no better way to set this position apart than by using video and featuring real employees. HubSpot is highlighting real reps and giving candidates a clearer glimpse into the culture than black and white text could ever provide.

Is it easy to write a killer job description? No, but it is the face you put forth to the market. Consider it a piece of content that is used in the sales process. The person you are selling to is the potential candidate.

CHAPTER 13

COMPENSATE AT MARKET RATE

NOW THAT WE'VE DISCUSSED how to make your position stand out, it's time to turn to a more mercenary topic: *compensation*. To recruit and hire the best, you have to both pay a competitive wage *and* build an attractive compensation package. In this chapter, I'll share how you can determine market rate for sales development talent. We cover how to structure compelling compensation packages in chapter 14.

From the SDR Metrics research I've mentioned earlier, we know that average compensation in the United States is as follows (see figure13.1):

AVERAGE SDR COMPENSATION	
Base Salary	$46K
On-Target Earnings	$72K
Base % | Variable %	64% | 36%

Figure 13.1 – Sales development compensation

There is significant variation regionally, with San Francisco, Boston, and Washington, DC offering some of the highest base salaries and on-target earnings. I should also mention that my research is weighted towards technology companies – which generally pay more generously than services, manufacturing, and other sectors.

To give you a feel for how widely compensation varies, consider these two examples I recently pulled from a national recruiting site.

▶ Company A is seeking a proactive self-starter with a track record of successful lead follow-up and ability to penetrate multiple executive levels within an organization.

Location: Cambridge, Massachusetts
Base: $45K
Total Comp: $78K

▶ Company B is seeking a sales development representative to drive new pipeline through outbound prospecting with a focus on setting demo appointments for the sales team.

Location: Phoenix, Arizona
Base: $34K
Total Comp: $48K

These two positions differ by 30 percent in base salary and nearly 70 percent in on-target earnings. Variation that large is far from uncommon. I've found five variables that most affect compensation:

1. Region (Northeast, Midwest, Pacific Coast, etc.)
2. Required sales experience (None, less than one year, one or more years, etc.)
3. Model (introductory meetings vs. qualified opportunities)
4. Average sales price (<$10K, $10–49K, $50K+, etc.)
5. Type of product (software, service, product, etc.)

Even within a single region, variation in the other four factors can swing on-target earnings by up to 35 percent. To provide baseline benchmarks, I've built a tool based on my research. You can download the SDR Compensation Calculator here: http://sdrbook.io/SDRCOMP. To dial in "market" compensation, you'll likely want to do some Googling, ask local recruiters, and check sites such as Glassdoor, Indeed, and PayScale.

Small increases in salary might not seem like a lot to you, but you aren't your ideal candidate. Brand, culture, and maybe even equity might matter to your candidates. But base salary matters, too. Think of it this way. Average student loan debt was recently reported as having crossed $30,000. A $5K higher base and lower on-target earnings might not seem that attractive to you and me.

> *But to a recent grad, a five-thousand-dollar higher base salary might sound like not having to worry about student loan payments for an entire year.*

Keep the candidates' perspective in mind. Yes, you're going to build a great culture, they're going to learn a ton, and this will change the trajectory of their careers. But yes, you also have to pay a market rate.

CHAPTER 14

BUILD ATTRACTIVE COMPENSATION PLANS

AS SALES DEVELOPMENT HAS GROWN in professionalism, so has the sophistication of questions asked by candidates. Don't be surprised if you encounter potential hires who—beyond inquiring about base and on-target earnings—ask for specifics on how variable compensation is structured. In this chapter, I'll cover compensation plans that attract and motivate (not aggravate) top talent.

Great sales development compensation plans have three things in common:

1. **CLARITY.** The core plan has no more than two moving pieces, and the nuances can be bulleted out on a cocktail napkin. If it takes PowerPoint and a cross-country plane ride for you to explain it to a rep, the plan is broken.

2. **PAYMENT CLOSELY FOLLOWS ACTION.** To be effective, the reward has to closely follow the desired action. Payment two or even three quarters after the fact does nothing to incentivize more of that activity. It also leads to a huge time suck as SDRs meticulously track to ensure they get every dollar owed.

3. **REPS CONTROL THEIR OWN DESTINIES.** This one gets a lot of push-back (*I'm looking at you, CFOs!*), but I don't believe that

reps should be rewarded or penalized for the skills/actions of others. This includes tying a large portion of incentive compensation to won business. SDRs can't choose their partnered account executives. Nor do they participate in the opportunity process. A large share of their income shouldn't be dependent on factors outside of their control.

There Is No "Standard" Plan

I've been trying for years to find the perfect SDR comp plan. Sadly, it doesn't exist. I've seen plans follow managers from company to company with wildly different results. I've also seen plans that were total stinkers on first implementation be re-implemented—a year or two later—with rousing success.

So what's the best way to build a comp plan that motivates? Because you've read this far into this book, you shouldn't be shocked to hear me say, it depends. In terms of a general rule, base salary should be roughly 60–70 percent of total compensation for sales development reps. Also, whenever possible, pay incentive compensation monthly. These SDRs aren't your angel investors. Don't make them wait for a payday. Make sure they are taking home incentive compensation each and every month. Based on the SDR Metrics research I presented earlier (http://sdrbook.io/SDRMETRICS), we know the following:

▶ 80 percent of companies use one or two components in variable compensation.

▶ Roughly 40 percent of companies use "Number of Meetings Passed" to determine the largest share of incentive comp.

▶ Fewer than 25 percent of all SDR groups use "Number or Value of Opportunities Won" to determine the largest share of incentive comp.

As you can see in figure 14.1, there is a pretty wide variation in how plans are structured.

Largest Component in Variable Comp

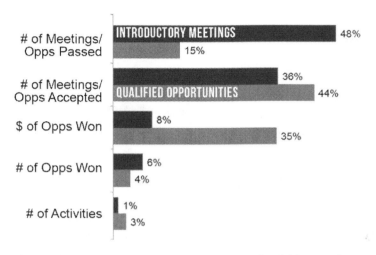

Figure 14.1 – What makes up the largest share of variable comp?

Let me share two specific approaches, the logic behind them, and what works well in each.

Approach 1: Pay on Meetings

For groups setting introductory meetings, you should pay them on meetings held. As you'll remember from part 1, for the introductory meeting model, you can't get much beyond *right profile*, *right person*, and *right pain* as qualification criteria. It follows that a rep's job is twofold. One, schedule the meeting. And two, make sure the meeting is held. Whether or not the meeting advances to the next step in the sales process is in the account executive's hands.

If you're worried about SDRs setting meetings with the wrong prospects, realign your *right profile, right person, right pain* criteria. If you're concerned over unqualified appointments, don't use the introductory meeting model. Don't confuse a strategy issue with an SDR issue. You can certainly pay a bonus or percentage of won business as a kicker for a job well done. But don't make it a large part of incentive compensation.

One final thought: you should absolutely use accelerators for this model. This means that the per-meeting commission before hitting quota is paid at a lower rate than is the per-meeting commission after hitting quota. Here's a simple example with three tiers for an SDR with a quota of eighteen meetings held monthly.

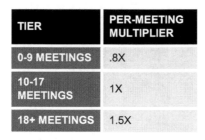

TIER	PER-MEETING MULTIPLIER
0-9 MEETINGS	.8X
10-17 MEETINGS	1X
18+ MEETINGS	1.5X

Figure 14.2 – Using accelerators and decelerators

So if the base commission per meeting held was $100, the eighth meeting would be worth $80 and the nineteenth worth $150. This is how you incentivize overachievement. This plan would also be uncapped—meaning no ceiling on monthly commission. As such, there is no incentive for an SDR to sandbag meetings (withhold until the following month) in an attempt to "game" the compensation plan.

Approach 2: Pay on Qualified Opportunities

For groups generating qualified opportunities, developing an incentive plan that motivates the right behavior and pays on both quantity and quality is easier said than done. I recommend the 50/40/10 approach. This plan works best with sales cycles under ninety days (more detail on why below).

This plan would look like the following (see figure 14.3):

BUCKET	% OF INCENTIVE COMPENSATION
OPPORTUNITIES GENERATED	50%
OPPORTUNITIES ACCEPTED	40%
OPPORTUNITIES WON	10%

Figure 14.3 – The 50/40/10 approach

So for example, a rep with on-target earnings of $50K might have an incentive pool of $20K. At 100 percent of quota, the monthly variable compensation would equal:

▶ $830 for hitting opportunities generated goal

▶ $670 for hitting opportunities accepted goal

▶ $160 from wins sourced

Senior leadership may be legitimately concerned about ensuring that reps have skin in the game in terms of quality. I think this approach is a fair compromise of quantity and quality—assuming a short-to-medium-length sales cycle.

For longer sales cycles, my preference is to pay more for opportunities generated (say 60 percent) and use the rate of opportunities accepted as a performance metric in career path promotion. I'll cover more about career paths in part 4.

For groups generating qualified opportunities, there is a strong impulse to equate quality with closed business. This often translates to paying the bulk of incentive compensation for closed deals that were sourced by the SDR. From a management perspective, this is couched in terms of "driving alignment with the business." From a rep perspective, they will often refer to it as "*screwing me for things outside my control.*"

It is my firm belief that you shouldn't tie more than 20 percent of incentive compensation to "opportunities won." If you have a complex sale with cycles running 120+ days, don't tie any incentive comp to wins. Think about it from the perspective of a brand new SDR.

Day 1, they start. Let's do this!
Day 20, they pass their first qualified opportunity. Woot!
Day 25, the opportunity is accepted by the AE. Awesome!
Day 30, nothing.
Day 60, nothing.
Day 90, nothing.
Day 119, the opportunity is closed and won. Hooray?

Are we really to believe that paying one hundred or more days after passing an opportunity drives any type of behavior? Nope. Finally, if you pay too heavily on opportunities won, your reps will turn into mini-sales admins. In order to make sure they get their deals over the finish line, they'll do all the back-office support work that an account executive might ask for. All the time they spend here is time not spent talking to new prospects.

CHAPTER 15

SOURCE CANDIDATES EFFECTIVELY

Let's pause for a moment to recap.

▶ You know the ideal traits for SDRs.

▶ You've created a job description that sizzles.

▶ You're committed to paying market rate for top talent.

Next up, you need to figure out how to source candidates. There are two broad buckets of candidates: *green candidates* or *experienced SDRs*. If you're hiring green candidates (those with no prior experience), you'll likely be posting on job boards, building referral programs, doing on-campus recruiting, etc. If you're hiring for experienced SDRs (those in an SDR role now), you need to take a different tack. Your mix of tactics will flow directly from the type of candidates you seek.

Green Candidates

To recruit candidates with no previous SDR experience, you'll want to spend time marketing the position. You might use a specialized recruiter with a relationship at a local university or with a veterans group. You might actively participate in career fair-type events or, better yet, make contacts at local educational institutions. Get in *before* career day, and you'll be the first employer to set the vision for what an exciting opportunity looks like.

Additionally, be sure to use inbound marketing principles in your posts on job boards. This can be as simple as including "recent grads," "for veterans," "entry level," or "business major" in the title of your job post and writing for those specific audiences. Re-read the Acquia example from chapter 12 to see what I mean.

Experienced SDRs

As with green candidates, you'll need to combine multiple tactics to attract talent. But in my experience, using job boards to source top candidates with six to twelve months of relevant experience offers little return. To be successful, you're going to need to get in front of these reps and to pitch them on the proposition that *the best* path toward their end game (a closing role, founding a company, marketing, leadership, etc.) is by joining you for a fantastic learning and growth experience.

Unless you are that rare shining company on a hill (e.g., Google, Salesforce, Twitter), you'll need to drive top candidates to your door. This means going after passive candidates—those who are currently employed and not actively searching for other positions. The two most important components of "activating" passive candidates are *the messenger* and *the ask*.

▶ **THE MESSENGER:** For a passive candidate strategy to work, who sends the message is sometimes more important than what's in the message itself. Think of it this way. You yourself are likely receiving messages from recruiters on LinkedIn. Many follow this script: "I came across your profile and wanted to see if you would be interested in a ____ role?" When you get a message like that, do you jump up, high-five a passerby, and shoot off an enthusiastic reply? I suspect not. But how would you react if the CEO, the SVP of sales, or another senior hiring manager messaged you directly? Don't you think that would have a bigger impact on you? Everyone, even those early in their careers, expects to get hit up by recruiters on LinkedIn. You have to do the unexpected to stand out. Putting the right messenger in play is often a stand-out strategy.

▶ **THE ASK:** Think back to all those boilerplate recruiter messages flying around on LinkedIn. Beyond being nearly identical, they all tend to make one more fatal error. *They try to sell the role, not a conversation.* "If you are interested, please email me your résumé" will nearly always turn off a passive candidate. Can you imagine why? Because it sounds like work. The likelihood of going from not looking (no extra effort) to working on a résumé (actual work) is near zero. Messaging a passive candidate is about one thing: selling the next step. That next step should be either a reply or maybe a five-minute phone conversation on the candidate's commute home.

I've found three tactics that top all others for sourcing passive candidates. It's likely you're using at least one of these today. Deploying all three together is the most effective method for filling your candidate pipeline. The trifecta includes the following:

1. LinkedIn + Messenger + Ask

2. Prompting Employee Referrals

3. Setting a Networking Quota

Tactic 1: LinkedIn + Messenger + Ask

LinkedIn is by far the easiest way to get a message in front of someone when you don't know his or her email address. Once you've built a list of passive candidates, use this formula as a starting point for messaging them:

Stand-out subject, short and sweet, and sell the next step.

Remember our friends The Five Whys (see figure 15.1)?

Figure 15.1 – The Five Whys framework

Well, you have very similar hurdles to move a passive candidate to active status. To address *WHY LISTEN*, your subject line is key. With *WHY CARE*, the messenger and the ask come into play. Remember, most candidates don't receive messages from a future boss every day. Use that to your advantage. Play to their ego and court them.

Once you have their attention, sell the next step. Your call to action should be direct and low impact. Asking for a one-line reply is a softer touch than asking for a five-minute phone call and miles better than directing them to fill out an application.

Kevin Gaither is VP of sales for ZipRecruiter. He advises hiring managers to do the following: "Nail your subject line. Use their name, use where they went to school, use something that is specifically about them. Next, be specific about why you're reaching out and provide links to videos, great press, etc. Finally, ask for a referral (to another potential candidate) in case they aren't willing to consider a change. I've had tremendous success with a 'you or somebody you know' approach."

What a "great" message looks like is largely in the eye of the beholder. But I do want to share a few examples with you—one *so-so* and two *stellar*. The first is the standard recruiter LinkedIn message. You've seen it, I've seen it, and (no doubt) your candidates have seen it, too. I've used the second and third with my clients to great effect. The styles are widely different, but it should give you a good sense for what is working today.

Boilerplate Recruiter Message
Subject: Boston Inside Sales Networking

Hi Kyle,

My name is Joe Recruiter, and I'm a sales specialist with [COMPANY] in Boston. I came across your profile today and saw that you have great SDR experience.

I wanted to connect with sales professionals, like yourself, and network with you. If you are interested, I'd love to speak with you to learn more about your current responsibilities, interests, and future goals.

I appreciate your time and look forward to hearing back from you.

Customized One-to-Many Message
Subject: Austin SDRs Needed—Hot Startup

Hi,

I'm starting to expand the Austin office of [COMPANY]. I'm looking for SDRs like you with 1–2 years of selling experience.

[COMPANY] is a funded startup backed by [INVESTOR A] and [INVESTOR B]. Our CEO previously founded [BIG NAME COMPANY], which had a huge exit in 2013. This is a great opportunity to get in on the ground floor and sell in a very hot market.

Here's a link to learn more. Please pass the word on!

Customized One-to-One Message
Subject: Kyle, help me help you

Kyle,

With experience like yours (BA in marketing, top SDR at [COMPANY]), I'm sure you get dozens of recruiting emails weekly. Let me be direct.

I'd like to do one of two things:
1. Pay you a referral fee for connecting me to someone in your network with a background like yours who's interested in making a career change
   -or-
2. Schedule a call with you personally to discuss an SDR position at [COMPANY] and see if you'd consider joining our awesome team

Here's who I'm looking for: [LINK]. I'd appreciate a response either way and hope we can connect soon.

Compare the first "generic recruiter" message to the other two for just a second. Creating the one-to-many message (second example) takes only slightly more effort than the boilerplate one does, but it is so much more powerful! The one-to-one message (third example) will likely take a bit longer, but, heck, if you are going after those awesome passive candidates, aren't they worth the effort?

Tactic 2: Prompting Employee Referrals

Employee referrals are the best source for candidates. The trouble is that most teams aren't generating enough of them to fill their open reqs. Even organizations offering comparatively generous rewards ($1K+ for a new hire) suffer from a lack of referred candidates. The problem is that while cash is attractive, reps are too busy to focus on activating passive candidates in their own networks. Unless a friend or former colleague figuratively falls into their laps, the referral program rarely gets a second thought.

HubSpot's Mark Roberge, who earlier discussed how he made hiring his number one priority, shared the following approach with me. "I call this the referral. When a new rep has been in the role for three or six months, I tell them that tomorrow we are going to sit together for twenty minutes. And that tonight, I'm going to go through all their LinkedIn connections and find people that are early on in their careers at good companies. I'll build a list that we're going to go through together."

At the meeting, Mark will show up with a list of names to review with his reps. He shared that, upon seeing the list of names, his reps would exclaim, "Why didn't I think of these people?"

Your reps have a perspective that you can't get from LinkedIn or a résumé. That inside scoop can separate *"That candidate would be awesome!"* from *"Let's not go there with this person, as he is a bit of a nightmare."* Either way, you walk out with intel you couldn't gain otherwise. The value is in the employee referral, but the referral meeting is what primes the pump. Take action to get the most from your employees' networks. Prompting referrals—I prefer that over calling them forced—may just become your best source of candidates.

Tactic 3: Setting a Networking Quota

If you've taken my advice so far, you already have an "always be recruiting" mindset. If you are personally and directly responsible for hiring, one way to keep yourself honest is to set a networking quota for yourself. It needn't be "cold call fifty candidates a week" or "hand out flyers on campus two hours a month." But you should set realistic (and measureable) goals.

Phil Keene is the manager of sales development at TinderBox. In a post on the Inside Sales Experts blog, Phil shared, "I've made it a point to do a phone interview every single day—even when there isn't a hiring class or open req. If possible, I try to bring in a candidate for a face-to-face interview at least once a week. I also take a ton of coffee meetings with reps that want career advice. This allows me to recognize the best talent out there and be top of mind when they're thinking about making a career change."

So, are you overwhelmed yet? Well, don't be. If you run a sales development team, hiring is the most important part of your job. If the sales development organization rolls up to you, make sure your managers have adequate time and effective strategies for recruiting. Hiring takes significant time and effort, but having a team full of fantastic people makes every other aspect so much easier. This is an investment that pays off in spades.

CHAPTER 16

GLASSDOOR LIKE A PRO

I'M SURE YOU'RE AT LEAST PASSINGLY FAMILIAR with Glassdoor, the site where current and former employees anonymously review companies and their management teams (http://www.glassdoor.com). But have you taken a look at your company's Glassdoor reviews recently?

An even more important question: are your Glassdoor reviews helping or hurting your recruiting?

When looking for a new job, candidates are reviewing Glassdoor just like one would check TripAdvisor or Yelp for restaurant reviews. I don't know about you, but I rely on those sites when traveling to new cities. If a restaurant gets multiple bad reviews, it won't make it onto my shortlist.

The same holds true when people are looking for their next opportunity—particularly so for experienced SDRs.

Bad interview processes, micromanagers, sub-par compensation—they are all detailed out in the open on Glassdoor. I can assure you, great candidates are taking note of what they find there.

Take a look at these two reviews (see figure 16.1). Tell me, where would you rather interview?

COMPANY A(MAZING)	COMPANY B(RUTAL)
ABSOLUTELY AMAZING	**WORST MGMT TEAM EVER**
Pros	**Pros**
The entire organization, from product, to engineering, to C-Suite, is fantastic. It is exciting to be part of an org where everyone truly believes in what we do.	The people I worked with day to day were solid. Some of the products were top notch, while others simply can't compete with the big boys.
Cons	**Cons**
Typical growth challenges. Territories shifting, policies changing, etc. However, these challenges are dwarfed by how great it is to work with such a wonderful group of people.	3 CEOs, 3 SVPs of sales, 2 CMOs in 15 months. You get the idea. No stability at all is the main reason why this company is going down the tubes.
Advice to Management	**Advice to Management**
Keep up the transparency!	Get a stable management first, and then maybe the company can turn things around.

Figure 16.1 – A tale of two Glassdoor reviews

Take a moment to swing by Glassdoor and check out your company's reviews. I don't mind; I'll wait. Okay, now tell me, are you elated or agitated? If elated, good work! If agitated, do not despair. I'm going to share a few ways you can partner with others in your organization to right the ship.

Glassdoor Metrics

At the time of this writing, Glassdoor presents three headline metrics about companies. They are prominently highlighted on the company's profile and review pages:

1. Number of stars (out of 5)

2. Percentage who would recommend the job to a friend

3. Percentage who approve of the CEO

I've reviewed hundreds of company profiles, and there is wide variation in ratings. Here are examples at both extremes (see figure 16.2):

STAND-OUT COMPANY	FLAME-OUT COMPANY
4.6 Stars (130 Reviews)	2.5 Stars (82 Reviews)
94% Recommend to a friend	39% Recommend to a friend
97% Approval of CEO	49% Approval of CEO

Figure 16.2 – A tale of two Glassdoor ratings

In terms of a goal, you'll want to shoot for or above 3.7 out of 5 stars and 80 percent+ in "Recommend to a friend" and "Approval of CEO." I've spoken with dozens of candidates and recruiters, and that seems to be an unspoken line in the sand.

A Streak-Free Glassdoor

Would you work for a company with a hideous website? Probably not. It speaks volumes about a company if it isn't making an investment in branding and attracting prospects. Leading companies are giving that same level of thought and polish to presenting themselves on Glassdoor.

Far too many companies haven't even claimed their Glassdoor profiles. Their company pages are stock and bleak, and they present only the bare minimum of information. To stand out from the crowd, *spice it up*. Add pictures, videos, awards, information about your culture, your philanthropic commitments, etc. to your profile.

As an example, MathWorks has done an outstanding job with this. It's no wonder it was recognized as one of the "Best Places to Work" in 2015 by Glassdoor. Here's what it is doing right (and what you should be shooting for):

▶ Videos about the company vision

▶ Real employee pictures, not stock photos

▶ Highlighting core values and social mission

► Lots of employee reviews

MathWorks has created a window into the culture of its company. Now, not all of the reviews are glowing, but candidates can really get a sense of what the organization is about and what it would be like to work there.

Figure 16.3 – MathWorks: A Glassdoor success story

So how do you get from Point A (boring) to Point B (alluring!)? In short, encourage honest feedback. I've seen too many companies skip that middle word—*honest*—and suffer the consequences. Pressuring reps to be "team players" and leave faux-positive reviews is bad business. On more than one occasion, I've seen unhappy reps, shortly after departure, update their previous reviews with "My boss made me write that previous review; here's the truth." That casts a pall over every other glowing review. Just don't do it.

I recommend a three-step process for your company on Glassdoor: *encourage*, *respond*, and *address*.

Step one, encourage your current team to post reviews. Let them know you want them to have the best-of-the-best colleagues and that reviews on Glassdoor are one way to show what a great company you're building together. The most obvious times to ask for reviews are the following:

► Once you've claimed your company profile

► A few months into tenure for new hire

► At time of rep promotion or advancement

Step two, respond to any negative reviews honestly and non-defensively. Most likely, your HR folks will own the Glassdoor profile, but don't wait for them to respond. Get in front of any negative reviews and help to shape a reply. Also, be prepared to speak directly to those issues during your hiring process. Objection handling isn't only the domain of your reps. Step three, address the complaints. No, seriously. This is a way to build a better team, culture, and company. Reflect on the issues shared on Glassdoor, and try to fix them.

One of my clients, VISANOW, is an immigration service provider that makes the legal immigration process faster and easier. Kristy Nittskoff serves as director of talent development and has overseen a major turnaround for VISANOW on Glassdoor. When Kristy joined the company, the Glassdoor ratings were awful. Beyond just a blemish, VISANOW found that the negative reviews were hindering the recruitment process. Hiring managers would contact candidates on LinkedIn and receive replies like, "Thanks for reaching out. But I'm not looking." The manager would pry a little deeper and hear comments like, "After reading Glassdoor, I'm just not interested." Kristy knew something had to change.

"First, we committed to making a lot of positive changes based on the feedback. Not only did we make the changes, but I set the wheels in motion, internally, to let everyone know how important these reviews are," shared Kristy. "If a rep shares something great with one of our managers, even in passing, the managers will ask if the rep would be willing to leave that feedback on Glassdoor."

And it really worked. At the time of this writing, VISANOW boasts 3.8 stars and 78 percent "Recommend to a friend." If your company is where VISANOW was, your entire organization needs to know what the strategy is for presenting your corporate image to the world. Let your employees know that if they love their job and are excited about your company, Glassdoor is an excellent place to share.

CHAPTER 17

TREAT HIRING LIKE A SALES PROCESS

AS SALES LEADERS, we all tend to think we're great at hiring. *Who wouldn't want to work for us?* The reality is that the same traits we dislike in "cowboy" sellers—no process, go on gut, unpredictable—are the exact traits we bring to our recruiting efforts. We need to do better. I'm not suggesting you bring in aerospace engineers from NASA, but the hiring process does require some thought.

If you lack a defined process, you or your hiring managers are making decisions based on little more than gut reactions. "I liked her. Karen liked her. Gary said she seemed sharp. She seems like a good fit." But *why* did you, Karen, and Gary like the candidate? Did you even like the candidate for the same reasons? How do you compare your "likes" across multiple candidates?

Your recruiting process has to be just that, a process, and not random acts of hiring. In this chapter, I'm going to provide you with a six-step framework that I've built in my work with clients (see figure 17.1).

This process works extremely well for the majority of companies. Bear in mind, this isn't a rigid system. You can add steps or adjust to meet the unique needs of your organization. I promise not to take it personally.

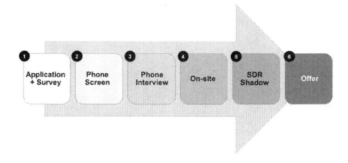

Figure 17.1 – Six-step hiring process

1. Application + Survey

I'm a huge advocate for attaching a brief web survey to your application. The purpose of the survey is to determine "fit" for your position and to quickly sort candidates into *yes*, *no*, and *maybe* buckets. At the risk of being presumptuous, you should put this into practice tomorrow.

In reality, screening résumés is time consuming and rarely gives you the full picture of a candidate. Great résumé writers can make bad reps or vice versa. A brief survey will allow you to quickly prioritize the candidates with skills closest to those you're seeking. The faster you can prioritize, the faster you can reach out, and the further ahead of other companies you'll be.

Here's how it works in practice. When candidates submit a résumé, prompt them to take a five-minute survey. There are several immediate benefits. First, the candidates *prove* they're interested by investing an additional five minutes. There are plenty of résumé blasters out there—reps who apply for any position with a pulse. They are unlikely to begin and even less likely to finish your survey. We've just eliminated them in one fell swoop.

Second, you'll see if they're able to do quick and effective internet research. A fair portion of the sales development role is web sleuthing. Why not test them upfront? Third, their responses will allow you to quickly bucket the applicants into *yes*, *maybe*, or *no* categories. You'll probably still want to review résumés, but the pile will shrink significantly.

When building the survey, I recommend a mix of open text and pick-list questions. I know I'm adding a step to your process, but I can promise you it won't take much effort, you'll learn about the candidate's ability to write coherently, and you'll save time by eliminating candidates without going résumé blind.

Here are a few sample questions to give you a feel for what this might look like.

Which of our products interest you most? Why?
[Open text]

Which two of the following do you consider our closest competitors?
[Pick list: include three competitors and three non-competitors]

In what year was our company founded?
[Pick list with correct and incorrect options]

If you had only thirty seconds, how would you explain what we do to someone you met in an airport/coffee shop/etc.?
[Open text]

These ideas are just to get you started. It will likely take a few passes to fine tune your questions. I'm confident that in the near term, you will be able to identify the best applicants and move them to the next step with speed. Even if you have external recruiters viewing résumés, have them use the survey as part of their process.

You might also prefer to substitute a commercial sales assessment (Disc, OMG, SalesGenomix, Talent Analytics, etc.) as part of your process. Feel free. Either way, you want to be spending more time evaluating great candidates and less time sifting through résumés.

2. Phone Screen

Our next step is a phone screen. If possible, have the initial screener be your talent specialist, recruiter, or HR person. For candidates currently in a sales development role, the recruiter can collect basic information: candidate's background, reasons for job change, what the candidate is looking for in a new role, etc. This step is about screening for red flags, not evaluating skills.

For green candidates, your questions will be a bit different. Find out if they've held relevant internships, done any phone-based work, have other applicable/related experiences, etc. If no red flags were uncovered, the recruiter should tell the candidate to expect a call from the hiring manager the next day. Make sure your talent specialist provides the hiring manager's name and title and sends an email to confirm.

3. Phone Interview

The third step is a more traditional interview, but briefer and still phone based. It should take no longer than twenty minutes and, hopefully, end by scheduling an in-person interview. When it comes to hiring SDRs, phone interviews are as (if not more) important than in-person. Your reps will be making their living on the phones. They need to be articulate and able to make a connection without being face to face. These are the first two questions you should ask:

1. What do you know about our company?
2. What do you know about me personally?

If the candidate doesn't do an outstanding job in responding, you should proceed no further. Great candidates will come prepared. They'll have used every means at their disposal to learn about your company, about your market, and about you the hiring manager. Not being prepared is a big red flag. In my experience, candidates who don't prepare for this conversation won't prepare for future conversations with prospects. And you need better than that.

Brandon O'Sullivan is an executive with a track record of leading high-performance sales teams. If you spend much time in the company of developers, you've no doubt heard mention of his company, GitHub—the site where developers can host and share code. I asked Brandon how he goes about making a great hire. "I can quickly identify, within a twenty-minute initial interview, whether I should bring the candidate back to meet the rest of my team," shared Brandon. "That's the real value of the phone interview. You are able to be judicious with your time, the candidate's time, and your team's time."

4. On-Site Interview

If your candidates have made it through the first three gates—survey, phone screen, and phone interview—it's time to bring them onsite. On-site interviews require real time commitments of yourself and your team. It is much better to disqualify aggressively in steps one through three and save cycles for all involved.

> First, a quick word of warning: if you schedule yourself or a team member to participate in an interview, you have to show up on time. No "something came up," no "a call ran long," no exceptions.
>
> Your candidate is looking for red flags, too. If people can't show up on time to make a good first impression, it suggests they don't really care about the candidate and/or the position.
>
> Candidates tell me this happens all the time. Be warned: top talent doesn't miss these signals.

Okay, back to the on-site interview. Building on the phone screen, you'll want to evaluate the candidates' ability to take in new information. During the phone interview, they were asked what they know about your company. Now, take it one level deeper. Probe them on what they know about your product and your market.

If you have trials, demos, or webinars available, ask them if they looked at them and about their impressions. Ask them what they've gleaned about your prospects and your target market. They don't have to be flawlessly prepared, but you should feel that they have made an investment. If they haven't, it suggests they lack curiosity and interest.

Now, on to the behavioral interview portion. The concept of behavioral interviewing is that how people have behaved in the past tells you a lot more about what they're going to do in the future than asking them to answer hypotheticals does. The internet is full of canned responses to common "How would you handle . . ." interview questions. Behavioral questions ask candidates to share specific examples of how they've performed in past situations.

ZipRecruiter's Kevin Gaither, who earlier shared his approach for sending LinkedIn messages to candidates, commented, "Too many managers ask questions about how someone would handle something. To me, that's just a BS way of trying to get at the answer, because how they would respond is not nearly as important as how they have responded in the past. I'm not looking for textbook answers. I'm looking for real stories."

So many candidates are asked the exact same questions in the interview process that their responses are rehearsed. This style is a bit different, and not all candidates will be familiar or comfortable with these types of questions. You might have to set the stage for them. For example, when asking about a time they struggled to learn a new skill, you might prompt them with the following:

- ▶ In what situation did you have to learn a new skill?
- ▶ When exactly was that?
- ▶ Why was learning the skill important to you?
- ▶ What was your process?
- ▶ What was the final outcome?

At this point, the candidate should understand what you are looking for. You want candidates who answer concisely, stay on point, and deliver a beginning, middle, and end. Try to eliminate as many yes or no questions as possible because they are conversation killers. I'm sure you have a list of trusted questions that you always turn to. By all means use them. Just keep in mind that behavioral questions help develop a fuller picture of the candidate. Make sure to weave a few into your process.

Finally, make sure to focus on the candidate's ability to ask you for something, more commonly referred to as "the close." At the risk of stating the obvious, closing is a critical sales development skill. If a candidate doesn't close at the end of the interview, you have a problem. It doesn't have to be perfect, especially if you're hiring green candidates, but it should seem natural for them. Their close can range from "Based on what you learned about me, are there concerns I can address right now?" to "Considering what we've talked about, how do I compare to your current team?" or even "What's the next step in the process?" or more cheekily, "How soon would you like me to start?"

The point is they can't just sail out the door without closing. Don't be afraid to be honest with them when they do close. There's no better time to test their objection-handling skills.

5. SDR Shadow

Because you have the candidate onsite, I highly recommend you give him or her an opportunity to sit with a current rep to see the job firsthand and ask candid questions. You want the candidate to feel comfortable asking questions such as the following:

- ▶ What is it really like here?

- ▶ What is the worst part of the job?

- ▶ How many reps are making quota?

- ▶ How much training do you really get?

When selecting which rep to be shadowed, pick someone who operates by the book. You want the process your candidates observe to be as close as possible to the one they'll be trained on if hired. If you're bringing in lots of candidates, make sure to spread the workload around. Most reps will be more than happy to meet with candidates, but you don't want it to become a burden. After all, they still have a number to make.

The candidates who make the most of this opportunity are the ones you want to hire. They'll be the ones who are comfortable asking hard questions of a peer who knows the day to day. Ask your reps to be honest—the good, the bad, and the ugly. Don't have them sugar coat anything, as it will come back to bite you.

After thirty or forty-five minutes of shadowing, your candidate will have seen the role firsthand and have a much better idea of what it means to be an SDR. After the shadow session, meet your candidate again. Ask:

► What's your impression of the role now?

► Do you see yourself succeeding here?

► What seems like the hardest part of the job?

► What other questions do you have for me?

That final question is *the big one*. If the candidates don't have questions after this immersion process, you should be concerned. Their heads should be spinning with thoughts on how they'll get up to speed and learn everything they need to know. Not having questions means they're overwhelmed, overconfident, or ready to run. This is the moment of truth when you can truly gauge their interest in the role.

6. Offer

Take a look at some of the most highly rated employers on Glassdoor, and you'll notice a common thread: *their interview processes are lean*. Many run from soup to nuts in just two weeks. If you want your perfect candidate to choose you, you need to move quickly.

Here's my (admittedly aggressive) timeline (see figure 18.1):

STAGE IN PROCESS	DAY
RECEIVE RÉSUMÉ & SURVEY	1
PHONE SCREEN	2
PHONE INTERVIEW	4
ON-SITE INTERVIEW & SHADOW	5–8
EXTEND OFFER	10

Figure 18.1 – A ten day sales hiring timeline

That's ten business days from application to offer. Personally, I prefer the offer to come from either the CEO or the VP sales—as high as you can go. This is a final opportunity to make the candidate feel special. Just like with job descriptions, *add some personality and sizzle* to the offer letter. It is a sales tool, and until the candidate signs on the dotted line, you are still in selling mode.

Let me share a brief story. Recently, I was mentoring a soon-to-be college graduate, Leah. She had reached out to me on LinkedIn and shared her intentions to begin a sales career. Leah had identified a shortlist of companies and asked me to highlight the best places to learn and grow. She began her interview processes with her top three choices at roughly the same time.

Over the course of two weeks, she made it through several rounds at each. On day ten, here's where she stood:

▶ On step 3 of 4 for Company A

▶ On step 3 of 5 for Company B

▶ With an offer in hand for Company C

She accepted the offer from Company C on day eleven. When she called me to let me know her decision, I asked about her impressions of the whole process. She commented, "All three companies talked about how they were fast-paced, agile cultures. But only Company C proved it in their process. That's why I accepted their offer."

Take heed. You don't want your *process* to cost you a great candidate. Speed is in the eye of the beholder.

PART 4

RETENTION

You manage things; you lead people.
GRACE HOPPER
(Rear Admiral, US Navy)

The flip side of recruiting outstanding people is that they're a demanding lot. Now that you've built a team of A-players, it's all about engaging, motivating, and retaining them.

In this section, I'll cover:
- ▶ The distinction between managing and motivating
- ▶ How learning is the new coin of the realm
- ▶ The tripod of retention: coaching, development, and career path

CHAPTER 18

LEAD YOUR PEOPLE

OKAY. Take a breath. Nice and deep.

You've done it. You successfully marketed the role, screened for talent, and positioned your company as the gateway to a successful career. Along the way, you invested blood, sweat, and tears and (perhaps) gained a few gray hairs. Finally and at long last, you can relax, kick back, and congratulate yourself for a job well done.

Not quite so fast. It's time to gear up for what can feel like another full-time job: engaging, developing, and motivating your reps. The fourth element for accelerating revenue growth with sales development is *retention*. In this part of the book, I'll share strategies, techniques, and examples for maximizing the return on investment of each and every hire you make. I'll spend time presenting factors that drive reps to stay with a company—or have them speeding toward the exits.

Rep Tenure

It takes approximately three to four months to ramp a new SDR to full productivity. This comes from the SDR Metrics research I mentioned earlier. Ramp time can be shorter in an inbound environment or longer if targeting enterprise accounts or more senior-level prospects.

I also know—from that same research—that average tenure is between twelve and eighteen months. At first blush, that may seem respectable. But trust me, after what you just went through to bring them on board, it feels like the blink of an eye. Also, in many markets—Austin, Boston, the San Francisco Bay area—you can expect to cut that number in half. There are just too many companies willing to take reps with six to twelve months' experience and give them a shot at a closing role.

So we know how long it takes to ramp SDRs, and we know how long they stay. Productive time in the role is just simple math: tenure minus ramp time. On average, that's just eight to fourteen months.

While pretty decent for a Hollywood marriage, I'd wager there are older leftovers hiding in the back of your office fridge. Considering the investment you made in attracting and hiring these reps, the closer you can get to *twenty months in role*, the better your team's results will be. There are a handful of factors that drive rep tenure both up and down. Here's some back-of-the-napkin math to set expectations (see figure 18.1):

SDR BASELINE	8 months
"IMPRESSIVE" COMPANY NAME	Add 2 months
GOOD, POSITIVE CULTURE	Add 3 months
GREAT LEARNING ENVIRONMENT	Add 4 months
DEFINED CAREER PATH	Add 6 months
HIRING GREEN CANDIDATES	Subtract 2 months
CUTTHROAT COMPETITIVE	Subtract 3 months
SUB-PAR COMPENSATION	Subtract 4 months
NO SDR-TO-AE PATH	Subtract 6 months

Figure 18.1 – SDR tenure expectations

While all of these factors affect retention, in my experience the single biggest factor that drives average tenure (up or down) is the person managing the team. The difference between ten and twenty-month average tenures comes down to the quality of the sales development leader and the environment he or she creates.

Managers Matter

There's an old sales management joke you may have heard. A VP of sales turns to the new sales manager and offers the following advice: "*The key to sales management is sincerely caring about each rep. Once you can fake that, the rest is easy.*" Now, I don't believe the situation is quite so grim. But I do know that just keeping pace with the day to day drives many sales development leaders to act like *managers*. They spend the majority of their time managing lists, managing processes, managing technologies, and managing metrics.

A great many managers spend more time emailing and instant messaging their reps than sitting with them one on one. This makes about as much sense as trying to teach your child to ride a bike via text messaging. You need to be hands on.

That style of management simply isn't good enough today. There is too much demand for talent, too much awareness of the role's enormous value, and too many recruiters chomping at the bit to poach your best reps should they feel unappreciated or disrespected.

I suspect you'll agree that no one goes into sales management because of an insatiable love for back-to-back-to-back meetings, quarterly business reviews, and spreadsheet blindness—even though that is often what the job becomes.

But why does this happen? Because (more often than not) that is what executive leadership asks for. There are only so many hours in the week, and managers are given little time (let alone structure, support, and direction) to actually lead their people.

Tom Peters is an author, speaker, and big-time management thinker. You might recognize Tom from his best-selling books *In Search of Excellence* and *The Little Big Things*. In his e-book *First Things before First Things*, Tom writes:

> If the regimental commander [*think*: CEO] lost most of his lieutenants and captains [*think*: Directors and VPs], it would be a tragedy. If he lost his sergeants [*think*: First-Line Managers], it would be an out and out catastrophe. The Army is fully aware that success on the battlefield is dependent to an extraordinary degree on its sergeants.

Tom's point is that managers are the number one lever for engaging, developing, and retaining people. The challenge lies in getting executive leadership to buy in on the impact this role can have on the achievement of strategic goals. So how do you make this a reality?

To adapt a line from former General Electric CEO Jack Welch, we can preach that "*hierarchy defines an organization in which managers have their face towards the boss and their ass towards the reps.*" Feel free to leave copies of this book on the executive team's desks with this section dog-eared. Or you can actively work to sell them on this idea:

It is getting harder and harder to over-achieve goals by "managing" processes and tools alone. Sales development leaders need to spend less time managing things and more time leading people.

Leadership Today

Today, reps expect a learning culture, they expect to grow professionally, and they expect you to deliver in those areas. The best leaders live by the following:

▶ My top priority is to increase the skills of each rep and the performance of my team.

▶ To do that, I'm going to create a robust learning environment.

▶ I commit to growing the talent of those I lead and to ensuring they remain within the company as valuable contributors.

You might be wondering, *All of that seems a bit altruistic; what about hitting my number?* Absolutely, hitting your number is important. But I believe two things to be true. One, if you build up your people, they will over-achieve. Two, hitting goals for any fiscal year is a marker of a job well done. But changing the career trajectory for dozens and dozens of people is the measure of a professional life well lived.

EMC is a company that understands this. Its *EMC Sales Associate Program* (http://sdrbook.io/EMCPROGRAM) takes individuals looking to begin a sales career and, according to its program brochure, offers them "intense technology training, live lead generation preparation, and invaluable mentoring to get [them] ready for the future [they've] always dreamed was possible." Here are a few quotes from program graduates.

> "The Sales Associate Program offers an environment to learn, practice, compete, and establish a strong foundation that is invaluable to your career."
>
> "I was able to transform into a strategic sales professional that knows how to connect with customers, provide solutions to customer challenges, and execute in a succinct, efficient manner. EMC has given me the foundation and fundamentals to propel my career forward."
>
> "The opportunity here is endless. The resources available to you are endless. Enter the program as you are, and exit as a member of the most seasoned sales force in the IT industry."

EMC has an entire section of its *Careers* site aimed specifically at "Students and Recent Grads." As a company, it is committed to marketing itself as a place to learn and grow.

Groupon shares this philosophy. Its recruiting video *Sales Development at Groupon* puts this thinking front and center (http://sdrbook.io/GROUPONSDR). The video features real reps and managers and highlights the opportunities for professional growth at Groupon. Here are a few snippets that jumped out for me.

> "Being an education major and having no sales or business experience, I knew I could be successful here. That is what drew me to Groupon."
>
> "Not many companies will take two, three, or four months to train you. They'll take two, three, or four weeks. The genuine focus on your personal and professional growth over a longer period of time makes Groupon an extremely compelling place to start your career."
>
> "As much as you want to learn, they'll teach you. They give all the resources and development needed to be successful."

Building this type of culture isn't as hard as it may sound. I've identified three areas for engaging and retaining your people: *coaching*, *professional development*, and *career path*. Over the next few chapters, we'll dive deeper and take each in turn.

CHAPTER 19

PRIORITIZE COACHING

I RAN ACROSS THIS LINE from the EcSell Institute some time ago, and it has stuck with me:

Coaching is not a component within the sales manager role;
managing is now a component of the new coaching role.

To me, that is the clearest expression of what it means to lead a team. In part 3, I discussed making recruiting a top three priority. Now, let's look at what fills the other top slots. As you might guess, coaching is one of them.

I often find that the terms *sales training* and *sales coaching* are used interchangeably. They shouldn't be. To my mind, sales training is about teaching a new technique or idea. In training, you are sharing the fundamentals of new material—laying the foundation. Sales coaching is about returning to a topic that is "old hat" and elevating a rep's abilities higher and higher, incrementally. Coaching doesn't revisit the fundamentals; it dives into the weeds with observation, questioning, diagnosis, and accountability.

There isn't an executive on the face of the planet who doesn't agree that sales coaching is critical. Nearly every single vice president of sales you meet will heartily agree that coaching reps is one of the best uses of his or her first-line managers' time (*Vital! Paramount! Instrumental!*). But were you to ask those same executives for specific ways in which they themselves are freeing their managers to coach more, you'll likely be greeted by crickets.

Let's be honest; sales coaching is about leaders developing the abilities of their reps. That's a line item that doesn't show up on the balance sheet. The only way to make coaching a priority is *to make the case with numbers*. Only by demonstrating that an hour spent coaching has a higher return on investment (ROI) than an hour spent poring over metrics—or lost in yet another meeting—can we make room for coaching. We have to get everyone across the sales organization to make this a priority—to make it a part of the culture.

Let's turn our attention to two separate studies that lead to one conclusion: *coaching has a serious ROI*.

Return on Coaching

Last year, Steve Richard, chief revenue officer of ExecVision, and I surveyed more than 1,300 individual contributor reps. We asked them a number of questions regarding compensation, career path, job satisfaction, and (you guessed it) coaching.

One question was: *on a scale of 0 to 10, how likely is it that you would recommend a role on your current team to a friend or colleague?* You might recognize this as The Net Promoter Score (NPS®). In case you aren't familiar with it, it is a scoring system that buckets respondents into the following categories:

▶ Detractors (ratings of 0–6) are unhappy.

▶ Passives (ratings of 7 or 8) are satisfied but unenthusiastic.

▶ Promoters (ratings of 9 or 10) are loyal enthusiasts.

We drilled into the correlation between coaching and job satisfaction. Steve and I expected the results to show that those reps receiving more coaching were *somewhat* more likely to be promoters. We found that and then some. It became clear that *more coaching* led to *more promoters*. In fact, those reps who reported receiving three or more hours of sales coaching per month were more than twice as likely to be promoters as those receiving fewer than three (see figure 19.1).

COACHING HOURS PER REP MONTHLY	% WHO WOULD RECOMMEND COMPANY
<3 HOURS	22%
3+ HOURS	45%

Figure 19.1 – Impact of coaching on rep enthusiasm

I'm sure you'd agree that enthusiasm is *good*, but productivity is *great*. It turns out that reps who are learning and growing are happier, stay in roles longer, and (as it just so happens) outperform their peers.

The best data to date on the effectiveness of sales coaching comes from the CEB Sales Executive Council. You might recognize the CEB as the folks behind the book *The Challenger Sale*. In an executive briefing, the Sales Executive Council shared that the difference in quota attainment between groups receiving fewer than two hours of coaching (per rep per month) and those receiving greater than three hours (per rep per month) was 17 percentage points (see figure 19.2).

COACHING HOURS PER REP MONTHLY	TEAM % OF QUOTA ATTAINMENT
<2 HOURS	90%
2–3 HOURS	92%
3+ HOURS	107%

Figure 19.2– Impact of coaching on group quota attainment
Source: http://sdrbook.io/CEBCOACHING

Think about what an uptick of 17 percentage points would mean for your team. For a group of six reps, that could spell the difference between $18M and $21M in sourced pipeline after twelve months.

Let me drive home the main point of this chapter right here: making sales coaching a priority is a business decision. Coaching improves retention and performance. Those are tangible business outcomes that even the shrewdest CFO can't argue against. In the next section, I'll give you specific techniques that you or your managers can use in coaching.

CHAPTER 20

COACH TO IMPROVE

IT'S NOT MY INTENTION to get deep into the weeds on *how to coach.* There are entire books on the subject that have made stellar work of that. I give you basic coaching techniques in this section, though you can use other resources for more in-depth coaching *how-to* advice.

With any new venture, the hardest part is getting started. In working with sales development leaders looking to formalize (or form) a coaching habit, I use a tool I call the *DESK-TO-5C.* Think of it as a cross between a "30 Day Challenge" and "Couch to 5K" (http://sdrbook.io/DESKTO5C). The outline of the plan is as follows (see figure 20.1):

WEEK 1: PREP	Goal	Plan the launch
	Time commitment	~3 hours
	# of reps	0
WEEK 2: LAND	Goal	Pilot and adjust
	Time commitment	~4 hours
	# of reps	2
WEEK 3: EXPAND	Goal	Scale
	Time commitment	~7 hours
	# of reps	4
WEEK 4: CEMENT	Goal	Refine
	Time commitment	~8 hours
	# of reps	5

Figure 20.1 – Desk-to-5C program

I've used this approach to quickly ramp coaching efforts with great success. It breaks a big objective (more coaching!) into bite-sized chunks while providing clear guardrails along the way. Feel free to adjust to meet the needs of your team. As you do, I'd suggest keeping four principles in mind.

1. **DEFINE THE COMMITMENT:** What is your coaching goal and what are you willing to re-prioritize to make it happen? For example, let's say your target is four coaching hours per rep per month and you have six reps. That's about thirty-six hours per month (including the work of pre-organization and post-documentation). When you look at it this way, five days a month isn't too much of an ask for a top three priority. That leaves seventeen business days for everything else. So, let's stop right here and make some decisions. What behavior will have to change for you to meet that goal?

2. **CREATE A SCHEDULE:** Add the dates and times you'll be spending with each rep to your calendar. This isn't just for you. This is a public declaration of your intent to prioritize coaching. Make a copy available to each rep and to your manager. That schedule is now sacrosanct. No excuses—everything else you do is now scheduled around those coaching windows.

3. **MEASURE RESULTS:** Track how well you're doing against your commitment. If you are below 80 percent of plan, it's time to re-evaluate. What's the problem? Are fires cropping up? Is your manager not respecting the time you have dedicated to this activity? Are you not enjoying/not feeling comfortable coaching? Get at the root of the problem, and take steps to get things back on track.

4. **KEEP IT FUN:** Keep your session fresh by mixing up the coaching methods. (More on this below.) It's a dirty little secret in sales leadership, but coaching can feel like a slog at times. Varying the method and setting is one way to keep it interesting for your team and, equally importantly, yourself.

Keep Coaching Fresh

Now that you have made the commitment to coaching, you want to make it fun. Bring a little variety into the mix, both in terms of format (live calling, listening to recorded calls, etc.) and audience (one on one or team based). I'll briefly share some of my preferred coaching formats.

Recorded Calls

How often do you watch live TV? If you're a frequent DVR user, sitting through commercial after commercial can be excruciating.

In coaching, sitting side by side with a rep and listening to voicemail after voicemail is the equivalent of commercials. If you have a bad list, or the Fates are against you, you might spend an entire coaching hour and never hear a single live conversation. Recording calls is one solution. There are legal issues at play on whether you can record with just the rep's permission (one-party consent) or whether you need to ask the prospect for permission (two-party consent). Before you launch any call recording plan, be sure to check with legal on the laws in your jurisdiction.

If you live in a one-party consent state and you are not recording calls, you're missing a huge opportunity to increase the skills of your team. If you live in a two-party consent state and can't figure out a way to ask buyers for permission, then record just your side of the call. Recorded calls can be used in a number of situations.

- ▶ In group sessions, you can play back the call for the team to discuss and share alternative approaches.
- ▶ On their own, reps can self-assess and reflect on what they did well and where they stumbled.
- ▶ Reps can "hand raise" and request coaching on a specific call.
- ▶ Managers can do spot checks to hear how reps are performing in real situations.

Imagine the impact of a library of recorded calls. You'd have "perfect calls" to use as models for new hires as well as individual snippets that display excellence in specific areas (e.g., call opening, objection handling, and closing). Even if you can record only one party (your rep), some of these same benefits exist. Technology has made this easier than ever, and call recordings can be linked to the actual contact or lead records inside your CRM.

Side-by-Side Coaching

This is the most common form of coaching. It is done one on one and typically involves the coach listening in as reps make live calls. With side-by-side coaching, you can evaluate more than phone skills. You can see how reps work their lists, how they prepare for calls, their workflow, and how effectively they're using the tools and technologies at their disposal.

Keep in mind that side-by-side coaching ups the pressure on reps. It's like someone coming into your home with a clipboard and taking notes on your parenting skills. At first, reps can be a little off. But most get used to it, and many grow to thrive on the challenge.

If you recall, we met Brandon O'Sullivan from GitHub earlier in discussing the value of short screening phone interviews. Brandon and I discussed his approach to side-by-side coaching. Like many leaders, Brandon found it too easy to have other tasks crowd out his coaching time. That's why he decided to make a commitment. Brandon blocks off every Tuesday and Thursday from 7 to 11 a.m. on his calendar. During that time, he rotates from desk to desk listening in on people's calls.

"I learned that from my old Oracle days," shared Brandon. "My manager came to me one day and said, 'Okay, we're making calls.' I asked, 'We're making calls? What do you mean we are making calls?' Those coaching sessions were the most nerve-racking hours of my early career, but they helped form a foundation that I've never lost."

Getting specific feedback and discussing what worked or what might have been done differently is incredibly valuable. Making calls side by side gives reps the ability to execute, debrief, strategize, and immediately put new thinking into practice. One point worth stressing is that you want to coach all your reps, not just the ones struggling. There are two reasons for this. One, even your best reps have weaknesses. It's your job to help them to get even better. Two, you don't want coaching to develop a stigma. If you coach only reps at the bottom of the leaderboard, then anytime you are in reps' cubes, they'll be worried their peers will know they're struggling. You want coaching to be a positive experience, not a major stressor.

Group Sessions

Group coaching sessions allow for coaching the entire team. You could select a topic—say objection handling—and ask each rep to bring a call (or recall a recent time) where they handled a common objection. They come to the session prepared to share with the group. The group talks about what worked and what didn't and provides feedback. You then select the best call of the session and make sure it is inserted into your "Hall of Fame" for best practices. Rinse and repeat on a regular basis.

From a time standpoint, one-to-many coaching is an excellent use of time. You might even host a monthly roundtable and ask all of the reps to share what they learned that month, what got them excited, and what worked really well. You'll learn where your coaching is influencing reps, and it might not be in the areas you expected. Finally, you'll find that reps are more likely to adopt and embrace your coaching if they hear how your advice is working for their peers. That kind of endorsement is a big win.

Self-Assessments

Having reps assess their own performance is an extremely useful exercise. Self-awareness is the first step to embracing feedback. If you record calls, have reps identify two that they feel didn't go well. These could be calls where they failed to get the prospect's attention or perhaps failed to close on a meeting. Listen to the calls together and ask reps to share what they did well and where they think they struggled. Provide your feedback and be sure to document the conversation in the post-coaching notes to be shared back with the rep. At your next session, make sure to revisit that topic and discuss any recent similar situations. *Coaching is about reinforcement.* You'll need to circle back to the skills you are working on regularly.

Jill Konrath is a keynote speaker and award-winning author. I asked Jill how she advises managers to deliver coaching feedback. "Don't just sit in judgment. Ask, 'Where did you think you ran into trouble? What did you think went particularly well? When was that prospect really interested, and if you could make one change to that call to make it better, what would it be?'

"You need to get them engaged and excited about constant improvement. Then you can offer some simple suggestions. And make sure to focus on one thing to learn at a time. You know, it's like golf. If a clubhouse pro tells me to change my grip, relax my arms, and not release my hands too early, I can't perfect them all at once. But if they have me focus on just on my grip, it might take me a while, but I'll get it down."

Hot Seat

First, a rant. If you really want to be a fantastic coach, I'm going to tell you something you may not want to hear. You (or your first-line managers if you're the executive sponsor) need to make calls. I personally make at least ten outbound calls every day. I do it to vet technologies, to validate lists, to test new messaging, etc. The benefits of firsthand experience are amazing. Making calls should be incorporated into your schedule. If your team is receiving inbound leads, grab five cold leads a month. If your reps are outbound prospecting, grab a few accounts that haven't been touched in a while.

In those few moments of calling, you'll gain a renewed appreciation for the job your reps are doing. Also, and this is actually one of the biggest benefits, you get to hear how your prospects respond to your messaging. We all think we've crafted the most elegant and effective messaging and call guides. But until you try them out firsthand, you really don't know. It reminds me of an old home builder's joke:

The primary function of the architect is to make things
difficult for the builder and impossible for the repairman.

Be that rare leader who can say, "I know this works. Because I've tested it." But be human, too. Share your experiences with your reps. Tell them when you crash and burn. Ask what you could have done better. Getting coaching from your team will bring you closer to them and ensure they're more receptive to your feedback.

At the risk of beating a dead horse here, the benefits to coaching surpass anything else you can do—from compensation, to gamification, to the beer cart on Friday afternoons. If you want a world-class team, you (or your first-line leaders) need to provide world-class coaching. No shortcuts, no excuses.

CHAPTER 21

DEVELOP TO GROW

THERE'S A QUOTE that keeps popping up on LinkedIn and Twitter. It really hits home with me—partly because these conversations speak to the state of *leadership* in the sales industry and partly because they happen too infrequently.

THE CFO ASKS THE CEO, "What happens if we invest in developing our people and they leave us?"
THE CEO RESPONDS, "What happens if we don't, and they stay?"

I'm confident that, as a company, you invest in onboarding. If you are like most organizations, this includes corporate history and mission, products and market, and process and technology. These are important elements. But they are also table stakes.

Remember the Groupon recruiting video I mentioned earlier? In it, they weren't touting how well Groupon trains new hires on *how to sell Groupon.* Instead, they focused on the depth of support and breadth of personal growth opportunities.

Helping your individual reps grow their professional skills is a critical success factor for retention. In the previous chapter, we talked about how coaching is one facet of a learning culture. In this chapter, we're going to cover the importance of professional development.

Quick question: is all this sounding a little *soft* for you? If it is, I totally get it. Sometimes it feels like being a sales development leader is part coach, part warden, and part therapist. To be fair, I did warn you: you can't hit your number managing process and tools alone. Consider what SAP Chief Executive Officer Bill McDermott has to offer. In an interview with HubSpot's Emma Snider (http://sdrbook.io/SAPBILL), he shared:

> *As a leader, you have to deeply care about the people who follow you—not just in terms of what they can do for you or your company, but how you can help them achieve their dreams and aspirations in life. Workplaces shouldn't be prison cells—they should be places where people come to flourish and fulfill their dreams.*

If it's good enough for the CEO of a $19B company with 70K+ employees, it can work for you and me.

Developing People

To my mind, there are three avenues for professional development. I think of them as *meet, learn,* and *teach. Meeting* is about getting exposure to other parts of your company. *Learning* involves your reps studying to become more well-rounded professionals. *Teaching* requires reps to understand ideas so deeply that they are able to present them to others.

Compare that to the reality of most training today, which is focused on skill enhancement of the individual. The entire team is trained as a single unit with each rep receiving the same information. This is not optimal, as each rep has unique wants and skill gaps. Treating them as a group can be hit or miss. *Meet, learn,* and *teach* allows reps to build toward individual development goals. Here's how it works.

Meet

Suppose a rep is interested in getting into sales operations or product marketing someday. It might be valuable for her to actually spend some time with people doing those jobs inside your company. I'm not suggesting you let her attach herself to the hips of an unsuspecting coworker (nor should she park herself in people's offices or expect to sit in on board meetings).

Think about how great it would be if a rep interested in a career in demand gen got to sit in on a quarterly business review with the marketing team. He could provide feedback and impressions of marketing campaigns while learning more about what it takes to create and execute marketing programs. A win/win all around.

I am suggesting that you give reps freedom—say an hour a week—to sit with and learn from people outside the sales development team. Four hours a month is roughly 2 percent of a rep's time. And trust me, if they want exposure to another department, they'll get it—around, over, or through you.

Learn

Here's one idea for building a learning culture. Quarterly, select a business book and buy it for your reps. Let them choose hard copy, e-book, audiobook, or other—the format doesn't matter. You'll want to mix up the topics to keep it interesting. For example:

Q1: The book on selling that most influenced your career
Q2: A hot book on the industry you sell into
Q3: A new sales book selected and voted upon by your team
Q4: Something that you know your buyers are reading

Notice that half of these aren't sales books. Think broader view for their development.

Each quarter, assign a book club discussion date and get it on your reps' calendars. Instruct reps to come prepared to roundtable the top three insights they gathered. For example, you could have them read *SNAP Selling* by Jill Konrath, and their "homework" would be the three ways they are going to rise above the noise and get the attention of crazy-busy buyers. Or you could select *Just Listen* by Mark Goulston. Reps would share their top three takeaways on communicating with hostile or resistant people. You, as the leader, can then create an action plan for implementing what has been learned.

Remember that this isn't about making your reps better SDRs. (Well, to be honest, it is a little.) But it is also about helping your reps grow personally and professionally.

Teach

I know it's hard to give your reps the time and space to attend virtual events or the occasional live event. Many leaders panic when they think about taking their reps off the phone. But not you; you're playing the long game where it's all about eighteen, twenty, or even twenty-four-plus months' average tenure. *Right?*

That's why you should fund outside learning opportunities. Encourage your reps to let you know when they identify an event they would like to participate in. This might be a webinar, a professional meetup in the evening, or a paid email course. You should evaluate it and, if it fits into their development plan, fund it for them.

This may seem strange to you or me, but many reps (*especially those right out of school*) are hesitant to spend $50 or $100 on outside learning. Remember, the average student just built up a $30K debt that was supposed to prepare him or her for the world. Getting them to foot the bill for one more course can be a tough sell.

You can allocate a learning amount per headcount or give out the dollars as incentives. The important part is to make it a true learning experience for both the rep and your team as a whole. Require reps to present what they learned back to the group—nothing too heavy, something along the lines of four or five slides on the key takeaways. Here's what this approach gives you:

1. It keeps the reps focused on learning. They'll be looking for those nuggets they can present.

2. It allows them to practice their presentation skills—both in creating the deck and in delivering to the team.

3. Even if you were to say the same exact thing, reps pay more attention (and give more weight) to advice from peers than from "the boss."

One option I highly recommend is the American Association of Inside Sales Professionals (AA-ISP). This organization is fantastic. It hosts both virtual and live events specifically focused on inside sales as a profession. The AA-ISP is all about great learning, great networking, and great development opportunities. Joining is a small financial investment and will give you and your team huge value.

Use Contests to Keep It Fun

There are many inflexion points in the sales development process (reaching prospects, getting callbacks/email responses, closing on meetings, etc.). These inflexion points give you a great way to vary your contests. When it comes to contests, you have to be more than a one-trick pony. If you only ever run contests on *most leads passed*, the same people will likely win again and again. That can become demotivating for the rest of the team. Here's an example of a team-based contest along the lines of a *scrimmage*:

- ▶ Randomly split the team into two groups.
- ▶ The winning team will be the one with the highest *average* number of meetings per rep (so if Team A set thirty-two meetings with four players, their score would be eight).
- ▶ Encourage teams to share ideas and work together to raise the performance of each rep.
- ▶ Award the winners a team prize: a catered event, team jerseys with logos, a team outing, etc.

With this type of contest, one or two superstars can't win it (acting alone). Everyone needs to contribute. I guarantee you, the peer learning and coaching from a competitive situation like this one can't be beat.

At this point, I hope you're with me on the development leads to retention leads to revenue bus. If you take nothing else from this book but what I laid out in the last two chapters, you'll improve average rep tenure.

Coaching is an investment you make of your time. That's under your control. Funding professional development is an investment the company has to choose to make. It kills me how often companies will spend $150 per rep per month on a hot new "acceleration technology," but if you seek a fraction of that for a rep development fund, the return on investment needs to be justified nine ways from Sunday. Remember: "What if we don't invest in our people, and they stay?"

Good question—ugly answer.

CHAPTER 22

BUILD CAREER PATHS

HOW MANY MONTHS should a top rep remain in a role before seeking a promotion or job change? That was a question we asked in the research survey I mentioned in chapter 19. We asked the question to both individual contributors and sales leaders. How many months seems appropriate to you?

Ready for the big reveal? Well, here it is:

Management thinking: twenty-one months
Rep thinking: fifteen months

That's roughly the equivalent of you expecting your kids to move out by age twenty-two and them expecting to live rent free until their mid-thirties. Whoops! Clearly, there is an expectation gap here.

Ask just about any sales development leader, and he or she will tell you that building a career path is a big retention challenge. This is true for both experienced and green reps. In that same survey, we also found (and this really shocked us) that the median rep response was eleven months.

Said another way, half of SDRs expect to be promoted or make a job change in less than one year.

That is a pretty surprising point of view. What's more, we found that reps who had the shortest expectations for promotions, and whose company did not meet those expectations, were less likely to recommend the company to a friend. You can see the trend in figure 22.1:

SDR PROMOTION EXPECTATION	% WHO WOULD RECOMMEND COMPANY
< 6 MONTHS	7%
7–9 MONTHS	18%
10–12 MONTHS	37%
12+ MONTHS	42%

Figure 22.1 – Impact of promotion expectations on rep enthusiasm

One large cause of this disconnect is *overselling* during the hiring process. In an effort to "close the candidate," hiring managers will, often unwittingly, hype the compensation, hype the role, or hype the career potential. This leads to *winning* the war for talent, but at the cost of hiring candidates who, from day one, have unrealistic expectations.

Stephen DePaoli is senior director of sales development at Arena Solutions. He shared, "We may tell a candidate the story about the person who got promoted in six months, but we tell them that they could just as well expect to spend two years in the role. Doing a good job of setting expectations upfront prevents disconnects and the inevitable disappointments."

There are two sides to this coin. On one, being honest about the realities of career advancement is a must. But on the other, companies do have room for innovation around advancement and career progression.

Build in Micro-Promotions

To some degree, I think there is confusion in reps' minds between *new role* and *new skills and challenges*. There is a world of difference between "I want to learn and grow" and "I'm ready to do something different." As we discussed earlier, managers who create learning environments have happier reps and less *need for speed* when it comes to role hopping.

Will your company be able to promote SDRs to account executives in under a year? If not, you might be facing a big, hairy retention challenge. You should, however, have the flexibility to build steps *within* roles. For example, you might hire a junior SDR, promote to associate SDR, and then elevate to senior SDR. I call these in-role advancements *micro-promotions*. (Although I wouldn't mention that to your reps. SDRs take these advancements dead seriously.)

Micro-promotions should be built on a five- to nine-month cadence. The cycle should be ramp, achieve, advance, ramp, achieve, advance, repeat. There are two key considerations for micro-promotions.

Consideration #1: Promote on Achievement, Not Tenure

Micro-promotions have to be earned. I'm not in the habit of handing out advancement for good attendance. I suspect you aren't, either. Think about the key performance indicators for each role. Specifically identify one or two key metrics, and base advancement on those. For example, a promotion from junior SDR to associate SDR might be earned based on the following:

- ▶ Three-month quota performance:100 percent+
- ▶ Three-month opportunity acceptance rate: 65 percent+
- ▶ Peer mentorship of two or more new hires

Note that these are hard metrics. They are targets for reps to focus on and can be reported on and verified. Without hard business metrics, you can't escape accusations of unfairness and favoritism. *"I started before Lisa and Chris! Why were they promoted and not me?"*

Consideration #2: Embed Expectations into Hiring

During the recruiting process, share the progression path with your candidates. Get it out on the table early. An inability to connect the dots between the role being offered and their future success lowers their odds of accepting your offer. Eliminate concern upfront by sharing what you have built. Being able to discuss your advancement plan during the interview process is a significant advantage in a competitive hiring market.

You should strongly consider micro-promotions. They're relatively easy and just about free. The best SDRs have an "up or out" bias, so it is up to you to define the ladder and requirements for advancement.

Moving from Prospector to Closer

The most common career path is from SDR to account executive. For most companies, it is a natural transition from an entry-level to a mid-level sales role. That doesn't, however, make it easy. The jump in skillset from the SDR role (*prospecting and qualifying*) to an AE role (*challenging and closing*) is significant. Very few can seamlessly make the leap.

The micro-promotions we detailed above are a way to bridge the gap. Adding small amounts of incremental responsibility along the path can be a great way to vet an SDR's desire and abilities. You could have SDRs work on larger accounts, call higher into target organizations, or perhaps participate in demos or sales calls for the opportunities they generate. The important thing is that they have the sense they are learning new skills and are upwardly mobile.

Emmanuelle Skala is an executive who gets it. As of this writing, she is the VP of sales for Influitive, and in a video for OpenView Venture Partners (http://sdrbook.io/SKALASDR), Emmanuelle discusses when and how she promotes SDRs. "Frankly, an SDR can have hit their metrics and not have the skillset for the AE role. The things I do to make sure they're ready to be promoted are outside of metrics. For example, I will let them run a first call or let them run a small deal. I don't necessarily expect them to close it, but I want to see how they manage that deal."

Emmanuelle is looking for her SDRs to demonstrate that they have the traits that will make them successful account executives. Should reps miss that mark, it is critical to give them very specific feedback on how and where they fell short. Also, be sure to communicate that this isn't a one-and-done process. You might find that excellent AEs come from SDRs who took two or three attempts to demonstrate their readiness.

Let me share what the SDR-to-AE transition looks like in the real world. In figure 22.2, I've removed company and individual names, but the roles and timeframes are real. (Note: ASP stands for average sales price.)

	<$10K ASP	$25K ASP	$50K+ ASP
ROLE 1	Inbound SDR (5months)	Junior BDR (9 months)	Inbound SDR (8 months)
ROLE 2	Senior Inbound SDR (5 months)	Associate BDR (3 months)	Outbound ADR (4 months)
ROLE 3	Outbound SDR (4 months)	Senior BDR (7 months)	Enterprise ADR (12 months)
ROLE 4	Account Exec	Account Exec	Enterprise AE
FROM SDR TO CLOSER	14 months	19 months	24 months

Figure 22.2 – Real-world SDR-to-AE career paths

In terms of timing for promotion, there are a few variables to consider.

Average Sales Price Affects Promotion Timeframe

If you're selling lower-dollar-value deals with shorter sales cycles, your SDRs will likely be ready for promotion sooner. I've seen successful SDR-to-AE promotion periods range from nine to sixteen months. For companies with more complex sales, eighteen to twenty-four months isn't uncommon (with micro-promotions built in along the way).

Don't Rob Peter to Pay Paul

I would never advocate holding a rep back from promotion just so you can hit your SDR team number. But I'd also caution against letting your sales managers recruit away your reps before they're ready.

For one, it requires hard work and smart management to hit the company's SDR-sourced pipeline goal. It's doubly difficult if you can't elevate average rep tenure above six months. Finally, you're doing your reps a disservice if you promote them before they're ready. Your reps are more than "warm bodies," and you owe it to them to set them up for success.

Evaluate Internal Candidates Exactly as You Do External

I remember working with a company that had recently taken a large venture investment and had plans to double the number of account executives in less than a year. As a result, it promoted six SDRs to account executives in one quarter and planned to promote six more the next. It had one problem, though: each promoted rep had longer ramp time and lower quota attainment than account executives hired from outside the company.

One fact jumped out at me after I took a look at performance. Four of the promoted SDRs had fewer than nine months' experience before becoming AEs. Those reps *significantly* underperformed as account executives. An external hire was nearly twice as likely to achieve quota. However, the two promoted SDRs who had more than twelve months' experience before becoming AEs performed exactly as well as the external hires.

The moral of the story: *promote only those you would hire.* Put your SDRs through the same hiring and evaluation process you would for external candidates. No one benefits—not you, your company, sales leadership, or the SDRs themselves—when a promotion sets reps up to fail.

Give Them an Off-Ramp

I recently worked with a client who was experiencing massive SDR-to-AE attrition. The company had done a great job of hiring and making SDRs successful, but the reps were struggling mightily after being promoted to AEs. In fact, the failure rate of these promoted reps was double that of new hires from outside the company.

So we decided to build them an off-ramp.

We structured the career path with the hope of massive success, but also with the assumption that not every rep would thrive in the new role. At the ninety-day mark, those reps who are failing are given three options:

▶ Return to an SDR role
▶ Apply for another position within the company
▶ Be placed on a forty-five-day Performance Improvement Plan (PIP)

This may seem harsh at first blush, but this is much softer than just the path of warning, PIP, and termination. The new approach has been very successful so far. Several reps have already opted to return to the SDR role, and we've worked hard to erase any stigma. We've made it clear that reps can try again in the future and that the opportunity to become an account executive isn't one and done.

It's Okay to Leave Me and Stay with Us

The fact of the matter is that some of your SDRs are probably recent grads. In all likelihood, they didn't go to school with the burning desire to set meetings or qualify opportunities. It may be your company, your market, or your industry that holds the allure—not *sales* itself.

Is there room for growth within other areas of your company? Can reps transfer into marketing, sales ops, customer success, or sales management? How fabulous would it be to have someone with real sales experience in every department in your organization? Maybe your SDRs want to be closers. But maybe they're still trying to figure out their path. Can you give them options? Great talent is great talent—don't let them leave your building.

Let me give you three examples of SDR-to-non-sales-career paths. All three are taken from a well-known software company with a fairly large sales development group.

	SDR-TO-MARKETING	SDR-TO-MANAGEMENT	SDR-TO-CHANNEL
ROLE 1 (duration)	Junior SDR (6months)	Outbound SDR (9months)	Inbound SDR (7months)
ROLE 2 (duration)	PR Analyst (12months)	Sales Ops Specialist (20months)	Outbound SDR (6months)
ROLE 3 (duration)	Events Team Lead (10months+)	Manager, Sales Ops (5months+)	Channel MGR (10months+)

Figure 22.3 – Real-world SDR-to-other-career paths

If you can't build career paths within your organization, then you have to plan accordingly. Yes, attrition hurts, but it hurts a whole lot less if you've planned for it and taken all possible steps to minimize it.

PART 5

EXECUTION

If you went to a play and someone appeared on stage and proceeded to read the play—
with no acting—you'd say they missed the point.
TOM PETERS

You've built your strategy, segmented and specialized, recruited, and retained your talent. Now it's time to switch gears and get tactical.

In this section, I'll cover:
- ▶ Dramatically improving your onboarding experience
- ▶ The impact of cadence and media on outreach
- ▶ Voicemail and email frameworks that get results

CHAPTER 23

MASTER BLOCKING & TACKLING

IF YOU DID A QUICK SEARCH for "business execution," you'd find about a dozen variations on this quote: *Vision without execution is hallucination.* So far, I've seen it attributed to Thomas Edison, Henry Ford, Michael Dell, and George R. R. Martin. If I kept searching, I'm sure I'd find attributions to Abe Lincoln, Albert Einstein, and Alexander the Great, too.

The point stands, however. Execution isn't *lesser* than strategy. If our grand designs fail when put into practice, how grand were they really?

The fifth element for accelerating revenue growth with sales development is *execution.* To my mind, your sales development group's ability to execute comes down to three things:

1. The speed at which your reps ramp

2. How intelligently reps speak to prospect business challenges

3. Your group's effectiveness at reaching and engaging prospects

In this part of the book, I'll share strategies, examples, and tools you can use to accelerate onboarding, craft buyer-based messaging, and design effective outreach. I'll also share a handful of stellar and less-than-stellar messaging examples.

Efficient Onboarding

As I presented earlier, average sales development tenure is between twelve and eighteen months (with a three- or four-month ramp window). This leaves us with just under one year of full productivity per rep. In part 4, I shared strategies for improving retention and lengthening rep tenure. Now, let's turn our attention to shortening time to ramp for new hires.

When I speak with executives about their onboarding process, many will share some variation of this:

▶ The first few days are new hire orientation.

▶ Then we put them right into product and internal systems training.

▶ After that, we have them listen to live calls with some of the more senior reps.

▶ Next, we give them low-level leads to practice on.

▶ Finally, at the end of week two, we put them in the lead rotation and they're off to the races.

Think about that two-week plan. That isn't how people learn—not effectively, anyway. In our rush to get our reps productive, we're essentially bringing them in, telling them "Marc is good. Be like Marc," booting them in the rear, and letting them have at it.

This makes about as much sense as teaching someone to drive by having him or her it in the passenger seat for two weeks. Observation alone is great for being able to identify a good driver. But it's a terrible strategy for becoming one.

I have a theory as to why this approach is so common. We've just gone through a tough process to source, interview, evaluate, and recruit these new hires. And if we're being honest, we're a tiny bit fatigued at this point. We've descended from the Peak of Expectations (*I just hired an A-player! I'm awesome at this!*) and encountered the Trough of Hirer's Remorse (*They seemed so brilliant during the interview*). We just want to sprint straight up the Slope of Onboarding as fast as humanly possible to get to the majestic Rising Hills of Productivity (see figure 23.1).

Figure 23.1 – Manager expectations of new hires over time

But here's the larger problem: we're undermining the serious investment we made in hiring top talent with a *check-the-box* onboarding process. As a result, too many sales development reps aren't properly prepared to take the field.

How People Learn

Effective onboarding begins with an understanding of how people learn. Jill Konrath, an author and sales keynote speaker, believes that leaders misunderstand the best way to get reps up to speed quickly. "Managers will tell a new rep to get on the phone with John and listen to what he's saying. Or go pay attention to what Katie's doing because she's really good. But there's no connection between what this A-player does and how the new rep is supposed to get there. The manager pays no attention to transferring the knowledge and experiences that the new rep will need to be as successful as Katie and John."

Jill has written an entire book, *Agile Selling*, on this very topic. Jill shared with me that new reps learn most effectively when the approach involves *chunking*, *sequencing*, and *connecting*. Let me summarize what that means.

▶ **CHUNKING:** It's easier to learn a new subject in bite-sized chunks. When you overwhelm someone, information isn't readily absorbed. You have to break the material down into smaller, easier-to-absorb blocks. For example, learning about all the different prospect personas involved in your sale can be overwhelming. Expose new reps to each persona—one at a time. Paint the picture for how they relate to each other and form the org chart.

▶ **SEQUENCING:** Determining what comes first, in order of importance, is key to learning (think: logical building block). Decide what's essential to learn now versus what can wait. It does little good for new reps to learn features and benefits before they learn about prospect pain and the implications of the status quo.

▶ **CONNECTING:** This ties it all together. You've created a learning sequence built with bite-sized chunks of information. Now you need to connect the dots. Say your reps have just learned about prospect challenges and prospect personas. Now, help them link each prospect to the business drivers that resonate best with them. Then when you cover messaging, reps will understand the story behind the story.

How many of us build our onboarding plans with these three concepts in mind? We (as leaders) are in a great big hurry to get our people up, running, and productive. It goes against our instincts to slow down the learning. We incorrectly assume, *If shadowing top reps and role playing are good, then eight hours of nothing but shadowing top reps and role playing must be very good.* It's cliché to describe onboarding as "drinking from a fire hose," but it's also an apt description.

The reality is that as we pour and pour all this new information into reps' ears, the more and more confused they get and the longer it takes for them to get up to speed. If you take away nothing else from this section, remember this:

Keep onboarding sessions short. Make the order purposeful.
Let them sleep on it. Learn, then do. Revisit. And revisit
again. This is how people learn.

If you embrace these three principles, your onboarding will give reps both a clear picture of how all the different components tie together and a vision for how what they've learned will help them in the daily realities of their role. The good news is that great onboarding doesn't require a PhD in learning science or a team of engineers from Porsche to build.

Now that we've covered how people learn, let's turn our attention to building an onboarding plan.

CHAPTER 24

ONBOARD BY A PROCESS, NOT AN EVENT

CHARLIE BESECKER heads sales development and sales enablement for Qualtrics. He knows that the first two weeks with a new company create a lasting impression of what a new hire's tenure will be like. Charlie and Qualtrics started their onboarding program with a mission state-ment: *construct a meticulous, white-glove process.*

He shared, "Every new hire is given a schedule that covers their first few weeks along with *single-day schedules* each morning. Each one contains information such as meeting room, trainer, desired outcome of training, and any helpful hints. The training coordinator checks in with each new hire and makes sure they have everything they need and answers any questions they may have."

Take a moment to reflect on that. Imagine how that experience must feel for a new hire at Qualtrics. Now think about what your reps experience in their first few weeks at your company. How closely does it match the program Charlie shared?

What Qualtrics has done is truly white glove. That experience is what we should all be shooting for. *Someday.* But before we get to "white-glove resort," we need to get to "decent conference hotel."

In the rest of this chapter, I'm going to share five strategies and a sample calendar you can use to upgrade your onboarding.

1. Why before What

There's a TED talk from a few years ago that you may have seen. In it, Simon Sinek argues that we must *start with why.* "Every single person, every single organization knows *what* they do—100 percent. Some know *how* they do it—whether you call it your differentiating value proposition or your proprietary process. But very, very few people or organizations know *why* they do what they do. And by why I don't mean to make a profit. That's a result. By why I mean what's your purpose, what's your cause, what's your belief, why does your organization exist? And why should anyone care?"

This absolutely holds true in the world of sales development. Every rep— at least every respectable one—knows what his or her company does. Some (the good ones) know why their company is unique. They can speak to why a prospect should listen to their pitch. But the great ones (the rainmakers, the A-players, the elite) can speak to the bigger picture of why their company exists, why their founders decided to take a stand and say, "That right there. We're going to fix that." These reps are confident in why prospects should take notice and take a meeting.

Without understanding the *why*, reps struggle to connect with prospect priorities. Everything about the *what* and the *how* of a solution can be found online. So much of what a prospect needs to know about our products and services can be accessed with the click of a mouse. Our reps need to create value and offer insight and ideas that prospects can't find on their own.

We fall into trouble when we train reps on our products or services but never train them on our prospects' worlds. There are miles of difference between knowing that a VP of marketing "cares about lead quantity and lead quality" and understanding the professional and personal implications of missing a marketing-sourced pipeline quota. Here's a Tom Peters quote that I think sums up the problem beautifully:

If you went to a play and someone appeared on stage and proceeded to read the play—with no acting—you'd say they missed the point of theater.

If you teach reps about *our products* before they understand *their problem*, future conversations will be about products and not about the urgency of solving the problem.

This is exactly the situation we find ourselves in when we feed reps a steady diet of products, features, and processes. Our reps might know the right words, but they can't speak to the business drivers, motivations, and realities behind them. Help your team see the larger context your prospects are operating within. In figure 24.1, you'll find a traditional approach paired with additional context for learning.

TRADITIONAL APPROACH	ADDITIONAL CONTEXT
Mission statement	Why the status quo is broken
Whom we sell to	A day in the life of our prospects How prospects are measured/comp'd
Pain points	How prospects address challenges today With us/without us vision
Universal value proposition	Messaging themes by prospect persona
Call scripts and case studies	Sales development "toolkit"
Sales collateral	Content by persona

Figure 24.1 – Traditional and enhanced onboarding

The difference is quite stark. Here's one simple idea for ramping reps on a day-in-the-life of the perfect prospect: *let your customers do the talking*. Rather than give a presentation and handout on prospect personas, ask marketing (or sales enablement) to film a Q&A session with a customer or two. The video interview might cover the following:

► How would they describe their role?

► What was life like before our solution?

► Why did they tolerate the status quo for so long?

▶ What was the straw that broke the camel's back?

▶ How would they tell the story of what we delivered to a peer?

Putting *why* before *what* drives a completely different mindset. Now, when trained on products, your reps will understand how your solution ties into the needs, wants, and challenges of real-world prospects. This is a type of deep understanding that the vast majority of SDRs lack.

2. Leverage Internal "Prospects"

Do you sell into a functional area that actually exists within *your* company? For example, do you sell to *sales operations* and have a sales ops team within your organization? Perfect! It drives me insane that companies can have reps prospecting sales operations, yet their reps never sit down and ask day-in-the-life questions to their own sales ops team. You and your reps can stand around and spitball about what the sales operations role is like. Or you can walk twenty feet down the hall and ask them.

Get your sales ops team into a room with your SDRs. Ask them about their challenges and how they currently or previously solved specific problems. You and your team can take what you learned and develop very specific and compelling messaging. Obviously, this technique works equally well with sales leadership, marketing, information technology, human resources, or other internal departments.

I remember working with a company headquartered in Toronto, Ontario. It had a large sales development team, with half located in Toronto (supporting Canada) and another in Austin, Texas (supporting the United States). As you might imagine, there was quite a rivalry between the two locations—with the Austin team consistently having the upper hand. I was brought in by the Canadian VP of marketing to examine why Toronto was underperforming.

Both teams prospected into finance and legal departments. And Toronto just so happened to have both the *VP of finance* and the *chief legal counsel* in the office. I suggested that once a month, a Toronto-based SDR should take people from finance or legal to lunch and informally pick their brains. At the next sales development team meeting, the *lunch buyer* would share what he or she learned with the rest of the Toronto team. The results were jaw dropping. The quality of Toronto's voicemails, emails, and live conversations improved exponentially. For short dollars and minimal effort, they learned a ton from their colleagues about what it meant to be in finance and legal, day to day. In very short order, "Team Maple Leaves" overtook "Team Lone Stars."

I want to share another idea in this arena. Consider giving new reps some face time with your company's senior leadership. For a startup, this might be the CEO or a co-founder. For larger organizations, it might be the CMO or VP of sales. The point is that every company has a big, hairy vision for changing the world. But can most reps clearly articulate it? Probably not. Spending time with a senior manager to gain an understanding of why your company does what it does can be very motivating.

► Why are we in this business?

► Why are we important to our customers?

► How do we make a difference?

Aside from helping reps better understand your prospects, getting them aligned with the corporate vision serves another purpose: *retention*. Sharing your bigger vision is a way to bond your people to you. Tie the vision into why the sales development role is so important. Make that experience a key ingredient in onboarding, and you will have a more productive, loyal, and effective team.

3. Exit the Bubble

If your reps never exit the sales development bubble, they won't have the full picture of what it is that your company does. We intuitively understand this, but we tend to isolate new reps with peers and their direct manager. Onboarding rarely includes sessions with sales and marketing leadership or the executive team.

You might consider having new reps meet with someone in marketing with a demand generation role. Instead of learning about their challenges, the goal would be to understand the types of events, campaigns, and programs that marketing is running. Having learned about the relevant personas earlier in onboarding, new reps will be able to spot the connections among upcoming programs, target prospect personas, and appropriate sales development messages. Or have them sit in (silently) on initial presentations conducted by various account executives. Let them witness the outcome of the calls they'll shortly be scheduling. This will do more to grow their knowledge—and boost their absorption—than hours spent training on process.

4. There Will Be a Test

In theory, onboarding covers all the materials that reps will need to do their jobs. But when do you know if a new rep is ready to execute? Going through a series of formal trainings is a good first step. But to determine if new hires have retained the material (and more importantly if they can apply it in the real world), you need something additional. I recommend a certification process. By certifying reps, you apply a degree of measurement to your onboarding. You'll be able to test retention and identify areas for additional training and reinforcement.

In its simplest form, your certification should include the following:

▶ A focus on discrete chunks of knowledge

▶ Objective evaluations through proficiency exams

▶ A mix of testing methods (role plays, verbal, written, etc.)

▶ Confirmation that reps have made connections between the materials

It is best to plan for certification exams at relevant points throughout onboarding. The order should be classroom training, time to review materials, time to practice on their own, and then certification. Don't be afraid to have reps repeat sessions. Certification lacks teeth if everyone passes on the first attempt.

Just to give you an example, at the end of their first week, you might certify new reps on company messaging. You could give an oral exam with questions along the lines of the following:

QUESTION 1:	Why do customers choose us?
EVAL CRITERIA:	Can the SDR articulate 2+of:

- Generate more leads
- Close more deals
- Deliver faster, smarter customer service
- Make better business decisions

QUESTION 2:	Which trigger events create the need?
EVAL CRITERIA:	Can the SDR articulate 3+of:

- New sales leadership
- New marketing leadership
- High sales rep attrition
- Venture funding round
- Funding for direct competitor
- Major competitive loss

QUESTION 3:	What red flags identify a bad fit?
EVAL CRITERIA:	Can the SDR articulate 2+of:

- 12+ months remain on existing contract
- Bias for open-source software
- Under $10M in revenues
- HQ in Europe (EU privacy laws)

Notice that we're using objective measurement. In my experience, it's very difficult (if not impossible) to be subjectively consistent. If you don't have some type of objective criteria, how can you apply the same standard across days and weeks, or from rep to rep? Don't trust your future self or future managers to be internally consistent.

Make the certification as objective as possible. You might break certification into four models:

1. **Prospect-ready** (verbal evaluation of a rep's understanding of key prospects, pains, and with us/without us vision)

2. **Process-ready** (dry run of tool usage: CRM, content, other technologies)

3. **Message-ready** (provide a rep with several dummy leads; ask them to do pre-call planning and leave you customized emails/voicemails)

4. **Phone-ready** (a phone-based role play simulating a live connect)

5. Be Prepared to Break Some Eggs

It's worth remembering that next to no one is a star out of the gate. After all, there's a phrase for a successful newbie: *beginner's luck*. One VP of sales shared the following with me: "The key thing for leaders to remember is to get new reps on the phones ASAP. I'm not sure that there is a magic number, but I know that reps need hundreds of live connects before they are truly ramped. The faster they get there, the better."

It is my personal belief that reps should be on the phone making dials by the end of their first week. There should be short sessions woven in between classroom trainings, one-on-one meetings, and independent study. There is no better way to test their understanding than with live fire. Obviously, you don't want them calling *the best of the best* leads. But you do want them calling on real prospects. Let them make some calls on Friday afternoon and reflect over the weekend. You may be surprised at the list of insightful questions they'll return with on Monday morning.

I often give new reps the following advice.

It doesn't go crawl, walk, run. It goes fall, crawl, face plant, walk, stumble, run. Expect to screw up. Yes, it'll be humiliating, but you'll forget it in no time.

Combining these five strategies will shorten ramp time, increase new hire success, and help your people live up to their full potential. To close this chapter, I'd like to share a sample three-week sales development onboarding calendar (see figure 24.2). As you'll notice, I've incorporated the five strategies shared above. You can also find the template at http://sdrbook.io/3WEEKONB. Feel free to add, remove, and reorder as you see fit.

	MONDAY	TUESDAY	WEDNESDAY	THURSDAY	FRIDAY
WEEK ONE	Orientation & HR programs Welcome lunch with entire team (Afternoon) Read, highlight, and prepare questions on Playbook	Playbook training sessions Call shadow two SDRs Q&A + Set expectations for next day	Playbook training sessions (Afternoon) Call shadow two SDRs Q&A + Set expectations for next day	Playbook training session **Certification #1** Pre-call planning for tomorrow's live calling	1hr. prep & review with manager Live calling
WEEK TWO	Debrief with manager on Friday's calling Role playing (Afternoon) Live calling	Call shadow two more SDRs Lunch with co-founder & VP, sales **Certification #2**	Full day of live calling	Full day of live calling	Debrief with manager on calling Sit in on scheduled "Discovery Calls" Impressions, feedback, suggestions with mgr. + HR
WEEK THREE	Side-by-side call coaching with manager (Afternoon) Live calling	Full day of live calling Lunch with CMO	Competitive, objections, and customer story deep dive **Certification #3**	Live calling Present feedback on Playbook to entire team Team happy hour	Live calling **Certification #4**

Figure 24.2 – Three-week SDR onboarding program

CHAPTER 25

CREATE COMPELLING CONVERSATIONS

LET'S TURN OUR ATTENTION to the second lever of execution: *how intelligently reps speak to business challenges*. Robin Dreeke is an FBI veteran. He has studied the science behind relationship development for more than twenty-seven years and previously led the Behavioral Analysis Program for the FBI. In his recent book *It's Not All About "Me,"* he shares this simple advice:

> *Suspend your ego to get people to like you.*

Those might be the toughest eight words to follow in all of sales. Suspending your ego means teaching your reps to put what they want (and what they're compensated for) aside for a moment. It is about being genuine enough to break down the natural resistance that prospects exhibit when being contacted by a seller.

It is also damn difficult to do.

There's a familiar line from Dale Carnegie's *How to Win Friends and Influence People* that goes, "You can make more friends in two months by becoming interested in other people than you can in two years by trying to get other people interested in you." In order to spark curiosity and generate interest, your reps need to have great conversations. This requires actually being *interested* in prospects. Reps need to be fully fluent in prospect challenges, motivations, and status quos. In short, they need to use buyer-based messaging.

But 99.9 percent of sales development reps do the opposite. They call and email prospects with seller-based, ego-filled messaging. Here's what that sounds like:

> "I'd love to chat with you about your sales strategies . . ."
>
> "Just calling to touch base and see if we could get our calendars coordinated . . ."
>
> "I wanted to drop a quick note to see if you had the chance to review my email from a few days ago."
>
> "If you are not the right person, I would appreciate if you could point me to the right contact."

Prospects respond to these types of messages the same as you or I would: "No thanks," "Don't care," "Still no," and "Not on your life." Well, at least that is how they respond in their heads. To be more accurate, I should say they don't respond at all. Prospects are so accustomed to deleting these types of messages that they do it on instinct. Ben Haines is the chief information officer of Pabst Brewing Company. In an interview with ZDnet (http://sdrbook.io/PABSTBEN), he shared the following:

> *"99 percent of the calls [I receive] are, 'I'd like to know what your IT strategy is and how we can help you.' I just delete those."*

Clearly, more is needed. The key to rising above the competition is *buyer-based messaging*. With buyer-based messaging, your reps will:

► Differentiate themselves with messages unique to each prospect

► Speak directly to prospect concerns, priorities, drivers, and levers

► Generate curiosity versus sounding like "just another sales rep"

Creating this type of messaging is part "give a man a fish" (providing reps with baseline guides and themes) and part "teach a man to fish" (sharing a framework that allows reps to experiment and innovate). Let me share two examples of how you can create this type of messaging for your team. The first works well in support of targeted, outbound prospecting, while the second aligns more closely to inbound lead qualification.

Buyer-Based Outbound

The biggest competitive advantage your reps have is the team behind them. The combined insights, experiences, and wisdom of your entire organization is the single best enablement tool for a sales development group. Yet the vast majority of companies leave it to the SDR manager and individual reps to build their own messaging. One of the best ways to create, or refresh, buyer-based messaging is by pulling together a cross-functional team for a workshop.

The key to executing compelling conversations lies in leveraging the tribal knowledge that is floating around within your organization.

Consider pulling in a small team, including account executives (both inside and field), the SDRs, marketing, product marketing, customer success, and relevant "internal prospects" (discussed in chapter 24). You don't need a cast of thousands, but you do need representation from the parts of your company that are having the most conversations with prospects and customers. Before the workshop, interview participants one on one. Gather each individual's perspective on the ideal market for targeted outbound, on prospect titles and pain points, etc. Here are a few sample questions you can use in the interview process:

▶ What does a company in our sweet spot look like?

▶ Which functional areas and titles should the SDR team call?

► What common challenges do those prospects face on a daily basis?

► How are they currently addressing those challenges?

► How do we improve on the status quo?

The point of the interviews is to give each person space to share his or her unique perspective and for you to identify the areas of overlap. Don't expect to hear total consistency. (Trust me, it ain't gonna happen.) Use what you hear to create draft findings. In the workshop, present your draft findings to the group and work toward consensus. You'll want to present, *Here's what I heard.* Then re-work the findings by asking, *What's right? What's off? What's missing?*

The endgame of the workshop isn't messaging. To write messaging, you can't have more than one set of hands on the steering wheel. It's up to you to take what you've collected and distill it into a phone- and email-friendly format. Plan to walk away from the workshop with several prospect-specific cheat sheets to serve as the foundation of your messaging. They might look something like this (figure 25.1):

PROSPECT PERSONA: Head of Corporate Recruiting	
TARGET TITLES	VP or Director of: recruiting, staffing, or talent acquisition
HIGH-LEVEL OBJECTIVE	Create and execute strategy for meeting talent needs of the business
ROLE & RESPONSIBILITIES	Design and lead talent acquisition process Understand workforce planning and forecasting needs Proactive candidate generation
CHALLENGES & OBSTACLES	All manual processes Reliant on IT for technology needs Unclear "wants" from hiring managers Staying abreast of trends and labor laws

PROFESSIONAL SUCCESS METRICS	Time-to-fill for open reqs
	Candidate pipeline
	Cost per hire
	Attrition rate
RISKS & FEARS	Missing hiring deadlines
	"Goldilocks" hiring managers
	Being outsourced
CONSEQUENCES OF STATUS QUO	At the mercy of IT systems and legacy processes
	Not in the driver's seat
BIG WIN WE DELIVER	No more spreadsheets!
	Real alignment on perfect candidate criteria
	Hard metrics on "a job well done"

Figure 25.1 – Sample prospect persona cheat sheet

One final piece of advice on this exercise: *make sure to include your SDRs.* Remember "exit the bubble" from the previous chapter? This is a great opportunity for your reps to hear how others within your company talk about your solution. And for experienced reps, they've likely spoken to more prospects in the last month than anyone else in the company. Their input will be valuable. Now that we have covered an approach to making outbound messaging buyer based, let's transition to inbound.

Buyer-Based Inbound

For most organizations, no two inbound leads look exactly alike. One prospect might come to your site from searching and downloading an e-book. Another might come via social media and register to attend a webinar, while another might stop by a tradeshow booth. All of these prospects have unique ways they came to us. Where we go awry is when our process does not acknowledge that fact. Many times, our flawed process encourages reps to think "a lead is a lead is a lead." They open up their list, start at the top, and work their way down—leaving vanilla messages, asking vanilla questions, and having vanilla conversations.

Recently, I was working with a project management software team where this was absolutely the case. The team's small inbound group was inundated with leads. Marketing automation was doing a fair job of scoring leads based on fit and activity, but the conversion rates were still not where they needed to be. In working with the team, I found that *all leads* (be they tradeshow, "request a trial," or any other lead source) were being treated *exactly* the same way. In fear of letting leads go cold, reps were hammering through lists, leaving the same voicemails, sending the same emails, and asking the same questions.

On paper, the team was supposed to be focused on passing qualified opportunities. But in practice, the reps were encouraged to quickly "get to every lead." In short, they were processing leads and not prospecting for opportunities.

Ardath Albee is the CEO of Marketing Interactions and the author of two fabulous books, *Digital Relevance* and *eMarketing Strategies for the Complex Sale*. I shared this story with Ardath, and she was in agreement that similar tales are all too common. "I'm sure you get calls, just like I do, where a rep will say, 'I saw that you downloaded something from our website. I was wondering if you needed anything else.' Well, at that point, I don't remember what the heck I may have downloaded. They don't know what it was either, and they certainly haven't read it themselves, so there is no way to have a real conversation. So instead they'll propose a demo or ask if I'd like to talk to their salesperson because that's all they have to offer."

As an antidote, Ardath suggests creating campaign-specific call guides. "I advise creating 'CliffsNotes for Sales' for the leads that content generates. That way, when reps call the leads, they can have a focused discussion based on which specific piece of content the prospect engaged with. We provide them with questions to ask or points to probe about so that the conversation has value."

Think about what Ardath's "CliffsNotes for Sales" would have meant for my project management software client. Before a big industry tradeshow, for example, marketing and/or sales enablement could have prepared an event brief. It might have looked something like figure 25.2.

Think about how taking the time to create this CliffsNotes strategy will affect the conversations your SDRs have with your prospects. The message they leave and the conversations they have will be so specific and relevant to the prospect. They will truly stand out from the rest of the crowd with their generic "I know you stopped by the booth" mantra.

EVENT: Project Management World Expo	
EVENT DATES	January 15th – January 18th
ATTENDEE PERSONAS	Director Creative Services IT/Operations Marketing Operations
KEYNOTE SPEAKERS	David Allen (Author of *Getting Things Done*) Nir Eyal (Author of *Hooked*)
SESSIONS WE DELIVERED	Email and Spreadsheets Are the Enemy 3 Ways to Cut Down on Meetings 20 Lessons on Succeeding at Work & Life
THEME OF OUR BOOTH	A New and Better Way to Work
CORE MESSAGE TO ATTENDEES	Sales execs have always had a way for their teams to collaborate and to see what individuals are working on. CRM was the answer. Now you can experience those same benefits. Our project management software becomes your system of record and tells you how your team is doing.
POINTS TO PROBE ON	Are they missing deadlines? Are team members not on the same page? Are team members working on different iterations of the same document?

Figure 25.2 – Sample event CliffsNotes for sales

Pre-Call Planning

The two exercises above will lay a strong foundation for buyer-based messaging. The final component required to equip your reps for business conversations is *pre-call planning*.

Pre-call planning takes good messaging and elevates it to great with one-to-one personalization. The goal is to hook individual prospects with a process that scales.

One big mistake I see reps and leaders making is to assume that pre-call planning requires deep, detailed, and lengthy research. It needn't. I recommend an approach I call *3-C*. Reps should focus on quickly uncovering a few bullet points on the *Company* being targeted and the *Contact* being prospected and prepare a few *Conversation Starters* to weave into their messaging. This entire process should take no more than five to ten minutes. And it needs to be done only *once*. After your reps have gathered their 3-Cs, they should make a note in your CRM. When it comes time to make another call or email, they can reference their previous pre-call notes.

To give you an idea of what this looks like in practice, here are a few sources your team can use.

COMPANY	CONTACT	CONVERSATION STARTER
Google News	Prospect personas	Recent award, accolade, quote
News & events/investor relations	LinkedIn profile (language used)	Something they shared on LinkedIn, YouTube, Twitter, etc.
Financials/growth stage	Tenure + previous work history	Big trend in industry/role
Glassdoor reviews	Shared connections, groups, associations	Relevant research/customer stories

Figure 25.3 – 3-C sources for pre-call planning

I discussed this topic with my friend Steve Richard, my co-author on the individual contributor survey mentioned earlier in chapter 19. Steve is a big proponent of using research as a way to earn the right to have a conversation with the prospect. "Reps don't need to know absolutely everything about the prospect and company they're calling. They need to be armed with just enough to show that they've made an effort. Pre-call research is really about discovering the why. Why are you calling them, why should they care, and why is what you're about to tell them truly valuable to their business?"

Steve and I are in total agreement, and this is true whether you are following up on an inbound lead or doing outbound calling. Pre-call planning can and should be done quickly and effectively. Reps who are prepared with researched bullet points have better (and more) conversations.

The next time you receive a cold call, ask the rep on the other end of the phone, *What do you know about me and my company?* If the response doesn't impress you, hang up. It is unlikely they have anything valuable to share. I ask that question to three or four reps a week. I'm constantly amazed at how ill prepared they are to respond. Nine out of ten times, the rep will not have done 3-C planning and will be using the much more popular 0-C approach (which stands for "zero clue").

The key to success for your SDRs lies in their ability to rise above the white noise that is everyone else approaching that prospect. Make the investment in creating the process and tools your reps can use effectively, and watch the conversations happen.

CHAPTER 26

ARCHITECT YOUR OUTREACH

LAST YEAR, I decided to run an experiment. I tracked and categorized all of the reps who were prospecting me personally over a one-month period. In total, I found reps from twenty-three different companies trying to book meetings with me. *What percentage of those reps do you think made four or more attempts to reach me?* Before I share the data, wager a guess. Got a number in your head? Good. Figure 26.1 shares what I found.

NUMBER OF ATTEMPTS	COUNT	PERCENTAGE
1 ATTEMPT	13	57%
2 ATTEMPTS	6	26%
3 ATTEMPTS	2	8%
4+ ATTEMPTS	2	9%

Figure 26.1 – Percentage of reps by number of attempts

Just 9 percent made four or more attempts. Not even one in ten. And I can tell you that if I ran the experiment today, the numbers would only have gotten worse. To my mind, effective outreach means mastering two things: a *multi-touch cadence* and a *multimedia approach*. Cadence is the number and rhythm of attempts your reps use to reach out. Media are the methods they use (e.g., phone, email, voicemail, and LinkedIn).

First, let's turn our attention to cadence.

Multi-Touch Cadence

Research from multiple sources has confirmed what I found in my small experiment: *reps are giving up too quickly*. Studies have found that it takes between six and ten attempts (including at least four by phone calls) to properly prospect a given contact. Consider the following from InsideSales.com:

> The absolute bare minimum number of attempts to contact at least 50 percent of your leads is 6. The average rep's performance? Between 1.7 and 2.1 attempts before they give up.
>
> —Insidesales.com: How Many Contact Attempts (*http://sdrbook.io/6ATTEMPTS*)

So where does this leave us? If it takes six to eight attempts to reach a prospect, and your team is executing fewer than four, that won't get the job done. Sure, they'll connect with a portion of prospects early in the process, but what about what's being left on the table? How much of your pipeline potential is sitting untapped?

Multimedia Approach

In addition to executing a multi-touch cadence, reps need to vary the media they use. This should include the following:

1. Voicemail
2. Email
3. Other (ghosting*, texting, social media)
   *Ghosting is calling a prospect, hoping to catch them live, and not leaving a voicemail message.

Yes, I know that *other* is a bucket, not a single medium. But I want to emphasize two things. One, voicemail and email are equally important. Two, voicemail and email together are twice as impactful as all the rest combined.

If I've offended any "social sellers" out there, I hope you'll read on to hear me out.

Think about the reps prospecting you today. I'd wager that if you were to keep track of their cadences, you'd find that more than half don't use the phone at all. Yes, they'll use a multi-touch cadence, but it will pretty closely resemble this:

- ▶ Cold email

- ▶ Did you see my earlier email?

- ▶ Resending in case you missed my other emails

- ▶ It's not you, it's me "breakup" email

In a word: *ugh*. That isn't an effective process; that's drive-by prospecting. To create pipeline, your reps need to use the phone. An over-reliance on email leaves them with pen pals—not prospects.

Matt Heinz is the president of a Seattle-based agency focused on sales and marketing acceleration. He and I discussed how he thinks about sales development outreach. "There just isn't a silver bullet. It's not social. It's not email. It's not any one thing. The reality is more complicated than that. Reps have to use all these media in concert to be successful. I will say that the phone remains one of the most important sales technologies we have at our disposal. The difference between a spammy cold call and one that gets a meeting is relevance."

Results, Not Responses

Last winter, I was working with a life sciences company and its outbound team. The group was focused on setting introductory meetings at multi-specialty medical practices. Gail, the group's leader, had been struggling to implement a formal multimedia process. Some reps were pushing back, saying that "email had a better response rate," while another faction was calling the same prospect five times a day because the reps didn't want to let them "hide behind voicemail."

Rather than lecture the reps on why they were wrong (or bore them with research stats), Gail and I decided to run a contest. Reps could choose to join one of three groups, and the team that set the most appointments per team member would have lunch offsite with the SVP of sales. (That may seem small potatoes, but exposure to a senior company executive really motivated the team.) The reps took the contest dead seriously. The only rule was that once you chose your group, you had to follow the group's prospecting rules. The three groups were as follows:

► **GROUP 1:** Could only send email. The phone could be used, but only for calls scheduled over email.

► **GROUP 2:** Could use email and the phone but could not leave voicemail.

► **GROUP 3:** Followed a six-touch process with three calls/voicemails and three emails.

The contest ran for two weeks. *Which group do you think took the prize?* Before I share the results, let me offer a little more data. We also tracked the number of responses, which we defined as any live connect or email reply. Not surprisingly, groups 1 and 2 had more responses. Planning and leaving quality voicemails takes work, and Group 3 had fewer overall activities (see figure 26.2).

GROUP	PROSPECTING STYLE	RESPONSES PER REP
GROUP 1	Email only	88
GROUP 2	Email + phone, no vm	91
GROUP 3	Six-touch process	74

Figure 26.2 – Three groups by responses per rep

Having seen the response data, want to adjust your guess? Okay, time to spill the beans. By the week's end, the clear winner was Group 3 (maybe not a huge surprise to you and me, but a real revelation to the team). What's more, they didn't just win; they killed it. The full results are shared in figure 26.3.

GROUP #	PROSPECTING STYLE	RESPONSES PER REP	MEETINGS SET PER REP
GROUP 1	Email only	88	8.6
GROUP 2	Email+ phone, no vm	91	9.4
GROUP 3	Six-touch process	74	10.2

Figure 26.3 – Three groups by meeting set per rep

Remember the title of this section, *Results, Not Responses*? Well, sometimes it is easy for reps to get hyper-focused on *responses* at the expense of *results*. They know they receive more responses from email but don't scrutinize the fact that, on average, a larger percentage of them are negative.

After we finished the contest, two things happened. One, we decided the entire team would participate in the offsite lunch. Hey, they all did a great job. Two, the reps bought in to the effectiveness of a multi-touch cadence with a multimedia approach.

CHAPTER 27

FORMALIZE YOUR CADENCE

IT'S CLEAR that the more depth and rhythm of outreach, the better the sales results. However, the way this is done should not be left up to individual SDRs. One rep might send two emails and quit. Another might leave the same (or similar) voicemail once a week for two months. Without guidance, each rep does his or her own thing—either changing course too frequently or doing what they've always done.

Implementing a formal and consistent cadence is a must for your group. For your reps, the routine helps them master the game—taking away uncertainty around *the process*. They can be confident that *this cadence* is how the most successful reps do it. They know what to do, and their job is to execute effectively.

In figure 27.1, you'll find a sample cadence that consists of nine touches over fifteen business days. This example leverages the phone, email, and ghosting (a phone call with no voicemail message left). Social attempts and marketing-driven nurture aren't shown in this pattern, but they can be built in.

Smart companies are figuring out the optimal cadence for their specific market and even specific prospects. You might have one cadence for inbound leads and another for outbound into A-List accounts.

Figure 27.1 – A sample cadence

Let me share with you how one high-growth software-as-a-service (SaaS) company out of Atlanta runs its cadence.

SalesLoft's Cadence

Kyle Porter, CEO of SalesLoft, certainly knows about cadence. In fact, his company built a product that help sales development teams execute prospecting. Kyle shared SalesLoft's 7x7 cadence which includes seven attempts for each new prospect over a span of seven days. The pattern follows:

▶ **DAY 1-** Reps send a personalized email in the morning. Later that day, they'll reach out via phone and either connect with the prospect or leave a voicemail.

▶ **DAY 2-** It's a phone call with no voicemail.

▶ **DAY 3-** Another call with voicemail in the morning and then one more call in the afternoon without voice mail. So in the first 3 days, we've got 1 email, 2 voicemails, and 2 no-voicemails.

▶ **DAY 4-** It's another email.

▶ **DAY 7-** Reps sends a final email and try to be original and human. SalesLoft has found humor to be very effective in this touch.

SalesLoft has found that for their market seven touches in seven days works best. For many of my clients it is nine touches in fifteen days. Don't get hung up on the numbers, you will find your unique formula with trial and error.

When you hand your SDRs a cadence pattern you aren't putting them in a box. You're providing them a roadmap for success. Kyle shared that his reps are encouraged to experiment. They just need to track their results and come back to the fold if their variations are underperforming. In the next several chapters, I'll share several principles for building messaging to use in your team's cadence.

CHAPTER 28

INSTILL A LOVE OF VOICEMAIL

KYLE SMITH is a consultant on my team. Kyle was recently training a sales development team, and the company's vice president of sales, Marc, decided to sit in. At the end of a block on effective prospecting, Kyle and Marc had following conversation:

> **KYLE:** Marc, we've been talking about the tendency to over-rely on email. Can you tell us, in the last two hours, how many sales emails did you receive?
>
> **MARC:** [scrolling through his iPhone] Fifty. Maybe even one hundred.
>
> **KYLE:** And in the same time, how many voicemails?
>
> **MARC:** Two.

One out of one hundred? Or one out of two? Which odds do you prefer? As we have briefly touched on already, many reps are skeptical of leaving voicemail. They'll often object with

- ▶ I never get callbacks from voicemail.
- ▶ I don't know anyone who leaves voicemail in their personal life.
- ▶ I get a better response from email.

While these may be honest opinions, they are also irrelevant. First, the return call rate on a single voicemail is negligible. So is the likelihood of a first date ending in a marriage proposal. By that math, dating is a waste of time. The value in leaving high-quality messages can't be measured that simply. A good voicemail might link a pressing issue to your company's name in your buyer's mind. It might prompt a prospect to reply to a previous email (this happens all the time). Or, in the best case, it might warm up the call when your rep does connect live.

Second, have you ever run into colleagues outside work on the weekend? Were they dressed in their "normal" Monday–Friday attire? I suspect not. There are norms governing the workplace that are distinct from personal life. Voicemail is still used by the overwhelming majority of business professionals. We use voicemail in sales development not because the reps enjoy it, but because prospects respond to it, and even if they don't do so immediately, it is a great way to deliver a part of your bigger story that comes across as more "mano y mano" and a less robotic form of communication.

Remember, we're hunting for prospects. Not pen pals.

In the rest of this chapter, I'll share four rules and a host of examples that will help your reps launch into the sales development elite.

Rule 1: Be Different and Be Relevant

"People always ask me whether or not they should bother leaving voicemails. My response is yes—as long as they are good ones," John Barrows, sales trainer to some of the best names in the tech industry, told me. "Touching base and checking in voicemails waste everyone's time. But voicemails that are targeted, state a reason for the call, and share relevant information work big time."

John is absolutely right. As in golf (or just about any other sport), performance has much more to do with the player than the equipment. The key to a great voicemail is to be interesting, relevant, and human. Those are the voicemails that stand out and rise above the noise. What *great* sounds like will differ from situation to situation, but it most certainly means doing miles better than the boring, bland boilerplate of *I was just hoping to get thirty minutes on your calendar to discuss your [INSERT] strategy.*

You, I, and everyone we know get messages like that. And, for the most part, we all respond the same way: *delete*. This is the pattern:

PROSPECT: [Presses play]
REP: Hi, this is Pat Smith with SomeSoft . . .
PROSPECT: [Don't know you, don't care]
REP: I was just hoping to get some time on your calendar to...
PROSPECT: [Delete]

Your reps have to interrupt the pattern, stand out, and be interesting. Before prospects can respond, they have to actually listen. If you want prospects to listen, your reps have to first show that they're interested in *them*. One way to do this is to demonstrate relevancy. For example, your reps could reference something happening in their industry, with their role, at their company, or that they shared in an interview or on Twitter.

Think of it this way. If you turn on the news and they're discussing a hurricane in a neighboring state, you may or may not pay any attention. If you turn on the news and they're discussing a hurricane in your city, you'll devote your full attention. Voicemail is no different. Coach your reps to think, *What one thing about this prospect can I include that will get them to tune in?* Let's try this again.

PROSPECT: [Presses play]
REP: Hi, Dana. Congratulations of your recent acquisition of Cloud Partners. What a great way to expand your APAC presence.
PROSPECT: [Yup, we're super smart.]
REP: Many of our customers have completed similarly scaled acquisitions, so I know that one of the biggest challenges is merging Salesforce instances.
PROSPECT: [Yeah, that's going to be a bit of a nightmare.]
REP: I have a few ideas I can share on how others have attacked that very problem. This is Pat Smith with SomeSoft, and I can be reached at 555.432.1212.

See the difference? This message was relevant and specific to the prospect. The likelihood of getting a return call with this kind of message is significantly higher.

Rule 2: Be Specific with the Ask

Even the most amazing voicemail needs a strong *call to action*, or it's all for naught. Your reps have to ask for something very specific if they have any hope of receiving a reply. Compare the strong calls to action (top) with the weak ones (bottom) in figure 28.1:

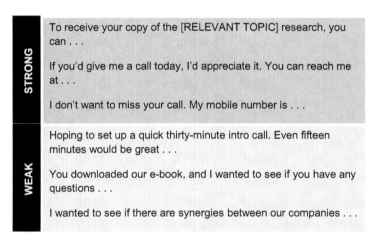

Figure 28.1 – Strong versus weak calls to action

Do you see the difference? The *ask* is much stronger for the top three. In the first example, the rep is making the prospect an offer of relevant research. In the second, just asking the prospect to call back "today" conveys a sense of urgency. Finally, the inclusion of a mobile number shows prospects they are important enough to receive special attention.

Rule 3: Don't Reference Previous Attempts

Prospects don't care that your reps made two other attempts. "Haven't heard back from you after my last call" and "Following up on my recent email" aren't good enough reasons to call again. Each message should build on the previous and offer something new. Referencing previous attempts wastes precious airtime and often comes off as hostile. That was certainly the case for this recent tweet from Steven Herod, technical director at Cloud Sherpas (figure 28.2):

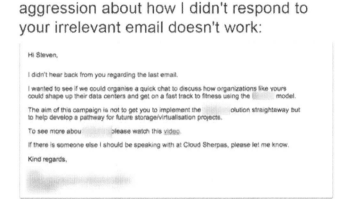

Figure 28.2 – Tweet from @sherod

Rule 4: Don't Trick Prospects

Never let reps leave deceiving messages. Too often, I'll catch reps leaving vague message like "Dana, Pat Smith here. Just have a quick question for you—555.432.1212" or being flat-out dishonest and saying they were referred by the CEO when they weren't. It may work; reps may get more callbacks. But you're setting a precedent that will have future implications. The line between fudging the truth with prospects and fudging the truth with my manager/company is wafer thin. In other words, if you let them get away with stretching the truth with prospects, how can you fault them for doing the same to you? For the teams I coach, the rule is *don't lie, don't BS, not even a little bit.*

Real-World Voicemails

Now that we've covered the four rules, I want to share some real-world examples with you—both good and bad. (Some of the best illustrations can come from *what not to do*.) Conventional wisdom tells us that the average prospect spends eight to fifteen seconds before deciding whether to continue listening or delete a voicemail. That's a very short runway to be different, be relevant, and interrupt the pattern.

As a rule of thumb, good voicemails run no longer than forty seconds. If you think of that window as super valuable real estate, think of the first ten seconds as Madison Avenue (Midtown Manhattan, NY) or Beverly Park Circle (Beverly Hills, CA).

It is my personal belief that reps shouldn't take up the beginning of their voicemails saying their name and company name. It wastes valuable real estate, and it makes them sound like everyone else. (Remember, be different!) The exception to the rule is the rare instance where the rep's name or company name actually helps. *Oh, Mark Zuckerberg from Facebook . . . I think I'll listen to this one.* Prospects are busy. If they don't immediately recognize your rep or your company, figuring it out requires effort. Plus, it is obvious the caller wants something from them, and hitting delete makes it all go away. Consider the following example:

> *Hi Dana, Pat Smith here from SomeSoft. 555.432.1212.*
> *Wanted to reach out to you and follow up on my email from*
> *last week. Hopefully you had a chance to take a look at it and*
> *found the information I had sent over interesting. Again, you*
> *can reach me at 555.432.1212.*

That message runs about thirty seconds long. But the preamble—name, company name, phone number, and following up—took up about twelve seconds and said absolutely nothing. Compare that to the following modified, and better, message:

> *Hi Dana, I'm calling to share with you a research report we*
> *just published on account executive retention trends. In it, we*
> *identify three strategies that decrease rep attrition by up to*

50 percent. This is Pat Smith at SomeSoft. To receive your
copy, you can reach me at 555.432.1212.

Now, that entire message took about twenty-two seconds to deliver. It targets sales leadership and focuses on a specific challenge many VPs of sales face. It hooks them with relevancy, makes them an offer of something of value, and comes in under twenty-five seconds. Boom! It will take coaching to hone your reps' abilities to leave succinct messages. Getting to the point without rambling is a skill. (If you need proof, just listen to any radio call-in show and try to find out what the callers are trying to communicate.)

Take, for instance, these two voicemails passed to me by a senior executive at a B2B technology company. I replaced the rep name and company name to save the guilty parties any embarrassment. As you read through each message, make a note of the point where you would have hit delete.

Example 1: 1 minute 20 seconds

Good afternoon, Dana. This is Pat Smith here over at SomeSoft. I'm the corporate account manager here for SomeSoft. My direct line is 555.432.1212. You know, I was reaching out to you today because I had something come across my desk that you had attended a webinar late last year in regards to looking at our application over at your company. Wanted to one, get in touch, introduce myself. I am one of two account managers who work on your account. In addition, I wanted to understand a little bit better possibly about some needs coming up this year and, if possible, if you wanted to get some more time with one of our client executives. So, if you have a few minutes, I'd love to hear back from you. If you have some time, we can set up a time here later this week or early next. My direct line is 555.432.1212. Thanks, and have a great day.

Example 2: 59 seconds

Good afternoon, Dana, Pat Smith calling from SomeSoft.

Just calling to touch base with you—see if we could get our
calendars coordinated for a brief high-level fifteen-minute
discussion regarding SomeSoft and your current antivirus
protection—speak to the value that SomeSoft can deliver
when it comes to antivirus and, you know, highly easy to use
antivirus protection as well as endpoint protection right out of
the box. Anyways, what I'll do Dana is send you an email.
My direct line here is 555.432.1212.I was looking to see if
we can get something on the calendar for the first or second
week of next month. But anyhow, look forward to speaking
with you and feel free to reach out to me at any time.
Thanks.

Hysterical, right? I'm not sure which one made me laugh more. Certainly,
these reps weren't prepared, and you can get a sense of how rambling an ill-
prepared voicemail can sound. But I also blame their manager, who hasn't
invested the time in developing a better messaging framework and who likely
isn't listening to their live calls to offer coaching feedback.

Here's the sad part. Those poor suckers show up every day and work their
buns off leaving those cringe-worthy messages. Imagine how much better
those messages would be if the reps had been given the four rules I shared
above.

Ready for some examples of what good looks like? To set the stage, let's
pick up from my earlier example. Say the SDR is prospecting Dana, the VP of
sales for a high-growth technology company. Again, the key is to be different,
relevant, and specific with the ask. For instance:

Hi, Dana. I noticed on your careers page that you're
dramatically scaling sales hiring. In this highly competitive
market, you have to get in front of the best talent before your
competition does.

Our clients have integrated video and social collaboration to
reach better candidates and shorten their hiring cycles. I'd
be happy to share with you how.

This is Pat Smith from SomeSoft at 555.432.1212.

Hi, Dana. In speaking with other VPs of sales, I know that the Boston hiring market for sales talent is on fire. Today's candidates expect extreme speed between first interview and offer.

In reviewing your Glassdoor reviews, it seems meeting those expectations is a challenge. SomeSoft has helped Company A (where I see you once worked) and Company B streamline their hiring processes.

I have a few ideas that might work for you. You can reach me at 555.432.1212. This is Pat Smith from SomeSoft, and my direct line is 555.432.1212.

I hope, by now, I've convinced you that with minimal effort your reps can leave stand-out voicemails. The key is to shift expectations from "getting a callback" (consider that a bonus!) to voicemail as one part of a multi-touch cadence that tells prospects a story of the value you deliver. That mindset (and the rules and examples above) will help your reps rise above the noise and dramatically increase their number of prospect conversations.

CHAPTER 29

ENGAGE WITH EMAIL

UNLIKE THE DEBATES, complaints, and at times tantrums over voicemail usage, convincing reps to use email is a pretty easy sell. The risk of rejection and humiliation is much, much lower compared to the phone. As a result, nearly every rep has a built-in pro-email bias. Thanks to technology, the cost of sending fifty (or even five hundred) additional emails is near $0. So guess what? *Prospects are drowning in sales emails.*

As someone who receives a lot of prospecting emails, trust me: *the majority of them are lousy.* In this chapter, we'll cover the three parts to sales development emails, and I'll share a host of examples.

The Three Parts

I can't remember where I heard it first, but a wise person once said, *"The best prospecting emails look like the letter F."* They are two or three paragraphs, open with something relevant and interesting, and end with a clear and short ask. They are direct and honest and can be read on a mobile device. Which of the following emails are you more likely to read? (See figure 29.1.) I've intentionally blurred out the content. I want to focus on how they look, not what's contained within them.

If you prefer A, then you're a better person than I am. Most people (myself included) don't "read" emails that are that long. Send us Email A, and we'll give it a skim. Send us Email B, however, and there's a real chance we might read every word. When training your reps, you want them to think in terms of three paragraphs—each with a specific purpose.

Figure 29.1 – A tale of two emails

1. **THE OPEN:** The subject and initial sentence are the first and only shot at keeping the prospect's finger off delete. Remember the ultra-prime real estate we talked about in the voicemail section? Well, the same holds true here. If we don't hook them with the open, it doesn't matter how well you execute the next two paragraphs.

2. **THEWIIFM:** This is the meat, where we pitch what's in it for them. What value are we offering? Why should they respond (let alone care)? Once again, just as in voicemail, the key is to get to the point succinctly, with personalization, and speak to a specific professional challenge.

3. **THE ASK:** This is your call to action. If the ask is clear and simple, the likelihood of responses increases exponentially. If confusing or requiring too much work, they won't.

Real-World Emails

I want to share a few more examples with you. These fall into the *what not to do* bucket. My goal here isn't to shame anyone—all of our reps make these types of mistakes. My aim is to deconstruct them and point out where they went awry.

Example 1
Subject: Meeting next week

Hi Dana,

My name is Pat Smith from SomeSoft. As you may know, the average sales rep spends over 4 hours per week updating CRM. We developed a platform that updates CRM automatically and helps you manage your pipeline and save time. I would like to schedule a 15-minute call to present SomeSoft and see whether it's a good fit.

SomeSoft helps over 10,000 users improve their win rate, including some of the world's best sales organizations: UPS, Oracle, and Thomson Reuters. Here are some of the benefits that SomeSoft delivers:

[Benefit 1]
[Benefit 2]
[Benefit 3]

You can read more about SomeSoft at www.somesoft.com and watch our demo. I would like to schedule a short call to show you how SomeSoft can help your organization. **Can we setup a 15-minute call in the next week or so to discuss?**

If you are not the right person, I would appreciate if you can point me to the right contact.

Looking forward to hearing from you!

So, what did you think? It is certainly . . . *comprehensive*. Let's review together. First, the message looks much more like Option A above than it does the letter "F." Second, the subject line is deceiving. It suggests a meeting is scheduled—not that one is being requested. If I opened the email thinking this was about a meeting I'd already agreed to, only to find out that it was a sales pitch, *delete*.

Next, the company name, SomeSoft, is used seven times. The prospect's company name is used zero. The message is clearly more about the sender than the recipient. The *what's in it for me* is boilerplate and totally lost in the mix. There's no role, industry, or prospect-specific customization. I'm not sure what UPS, Oracle, and Thomson Reuters have to do with each other—let alone what they have to do with a specific prospect. Finally, what's *the ask*: read more, watch a demo, schedule a call, or refer to the right person? That's way too many choices. If your reps overwhelm a prospect, they'll do what requires the least effort: *delete*.

Now that certainly isn't the worst sales development email I've ever seen. But the fundamental issue is that it fell victim to *show up and throw up*. There are probably three or four good emails buried in there. They should be broken apart and customized for one specific prospect.

Okay, on to the next one.

Example 2
Subject: SomeSoft Contact Information

Hi there,

I saw that you had downloaded some information on our SomeSoft portfolio and functionality. I am the SomeSoft account manager in your area, and am happy to answer any follow-up questions you might have.

I'd like to schedule some time with you to talk over some of your requirements. What does your schedule look like this week?

Thanks, and have a great day.

The good news is that this one is short. But, unfortunately, that's the extent of my positive review. Let's dig into this one. *Hi there* as a salutation: obviously the bare minimum of personalization was too much work. Using *you downloaded something so I'm emailing you* is an absolutely terrible opening. Why not be honest and say, "My manager makes me reach out to every lead to meet an SLA. I'm sending you this to just check the box and say, 'Yup. I followed up.'" *The ask* is so soft that it is almost non-existent. "What does your schedule look like this week?" Do they mean aesthetically, philosophically, or numerically?

If you want your team to write great emails, start dissecting those that you receive. Look for what works and what doesn't. In fact, ask every senior leader in your company to forward prospecting emails that they receive to your inbox. You want to see any that caught their eye, even if they didn't respond. This is a powerful source of sales enablement that 99 percent of companies are ignoring.

Let's dive deeper into what does work.

Paragraph 1: The Open

The best emails have subject lines that capture attention and flow beautifully into the first sentence. They also look like a real person wrote them and were sent one to one. No offense noreply@yourcompany.com, but we can all spot a "marketing email" masquerading as an email from a peer. Just this morning, I received these two emails back to back. One was sent to *look* like it was from a human (one to many), and the other was a normal email (one to one). Can you guess which is which?

Subject: **Go Mobile or Go Home [New Infographic]**
Hello Trish,
Google recently updated its search algorithm—they now rank sites based on mobile friendliness. In this new infographic . . .

Subject: **This is making you a commodity**

Trish,

This so-called "best practice" is bunk. I know from following you on Twitter that you agree that . . .

It's pretty obvious that the second email was sent to me personally—while the first was sent to me (and hundreds of others) having been "personalized" with my first name. Here are a few emails pulled from my inbox. Below each, I've shared how and why they caught my attention.

> *Subject*: **Your SDRs' voicemails**
> Trish,
>
> The vast majority of SDRs are boring the crap out of prospects with vanilla messaging. Are yours? And if you aren't listening to their calls, how can you be sure?

This one feels human all right. The subject and opening line look like they're coming from a peer—not marketing automation or a canned sales template. The language is direct (if a little colorful), and it certainly caught my eye.

> *Subject*: **Marc Benioff**
> Trish,
>
> Did you see the recent Benioff quote in Forbes [LINK TO ARTICLE]? It made me think of your blog post on . . .

This email used a name drop. This works well if there is a big personality in your industry—one that every prospect would immediately recognize. The sender then transitions to something that I had recently posted on my blog. That is how you capture and hold attention. Who doesn't love to hear about themselves?

> **Subject: Cambridge invitation-only event**
> Trish,
>
> We're expecting 50 CEOs to meet at Microsoft NERD on June 9th to talk about SaaS Sales. Care to join us?

This email used an event in my area to grab my eye. Everyone wants to know what is going on where they live and work. The first sentence is direct and relevant. The ask is crystal clear. I also like that they included the details later in the email. They tried to hook me on the what before they wasted any real estate on the logistics.

> **Subject: Triple your SDR productivity**
> Trish,
>
> Want to turn 1 SDR into 3? Our technology can do the dialing, so your reps can have three times more conversations . . .

This one went for the *wow* factor. The subject was definitely bold, and it flowed well into the opening paragraph. The big (and hopefully true) claim did a great job of grabbing my attention.

I think you'd agree that these three emails—each in its own way—stand out and interrupt the pattern. Have you received similar eye-catching emails lately? If and when you do, make sure to save them and share them with your team. Build a library of prospecting emails that combine a strong subject with a great first sentence to capture interest. Present them in a group setting. Assign "homework" for reps to go away and build a similar template for their prospecting.

I ran across a thread on growthhackers.com the other day (http://sdrbook.io/HANNAHW): *What is the best opening line you've received from a cold sales email?* Hannah Wright, who runs digital marketing at FormAssembly, shared, "An opening line addressing a relevant problem tends to grab my attention. Something straightforward and human. I remember at my previous startup, we were looking for interns and someone emailed me from a job board website. The opening sentence went something like: 'Hey Hannah, I saw that you're looking for interns—how has the response been so far?' They had either been scoping out other job boards or saw on social media that we were searching, but they knew we were actively looking to solve this problem and sent a very relevant message. Their email was only a few sentences and there was a question + call to action, making it tough to ignore."

That is the exact response you are going for.

Paragraph 2: What's In It for Me (WIIFM)

Here's where your reps have to offer something that matters to prospects. It's the value proposition, the thing that makes them realize you're worth their time. To get across WIIFM, emails need to tell prospects what you can do *for them* (not what you do). Let's return to an email we saw earlier.

> *Subject*: **Triple your SDR productivity**
> Trish,
>
> Want to turn 1 SDR into 3? Our technology can do the dialing, so your reps can have more conversations.
>
> I noticed that you're currently hiring for outbound SDRs. You mention they'll be making 50+ dials a day. Industry averages say that gets them to 7 conversations a day. Reps at other high-growth clients (using our tool) are having 20+ conversations daily.

Notice that the sender didn't lead with who they are or how their technology works. This email is an attempt to arouse curiosity and lead down the path to the ask. Email is about generating interest, not educating on what you do.

Paragraph 3: The Ask

The first two paragraphs have been leading up to this point. The ask is the next step your reps want the prospect to take. This should never be a throwaway. Let's continue using the previous example.

> *Subject*: **Triple your SDR productivity**
> Trish,
>
> Want to turn 1 SDR into 3? Our technology can do the dialing, so your reps can have more conversations.
>
> I noticed that you're currently hiring for outbound SDRs. You mention they'll be making 50+ dials a day. Industry averages say that gets them to 7 conversations a day. Reps at other high-growth clients are using our tool and having 20+ conversations daily.
>
> How can I get 10 minutes on your calendar to share more?

The ask here is clear: please reply with an answer to *how*. There's a raging debate around the "jump on a fifteen-minute call" request from a cold email. Some (maybe the majority) say go for it, while the other side argues that reps need to offer something of value before asking for time. They suggest asking open-ended questions or sharing videos or other relevant content to establish credibility. Once a dialog has been established, only then should a rep ask for a time—or so they argue.

I believe that the answer lies in trying both. Your reps are going to be sending a lot of email. Test both approaches, as there are many variables in play: name recognition, seniority of target prospect, recognition of the problem, prospect mood, rep selling style, etc. Remember, a great ask can dramatically increase the number and quality of conversations your reps can have. Don't waste it on something silly.

PART 6

LEADERSHIP

People leave managers, not companies.
MARCUS BUCKINGHAM and CURT COFFMAN

You mastered the first five elements. Now it's time to focus on day-to-day leadership.

In this section, I'll cover:
- ▶ Putting the right leader in charge
- ▶ Setting quotas, building processes, and measuring what matters
- ▶ The sales development technology stack

CHAPTER 30

CHOOSE THE RIGHT CAPTAIN

THE SIXTH AND FINAL ELEMENT for accelerating revenue growth with sales development is *leadership*. The book *First, Break All the Rules* gave us the great line "people leave managers, not companies." It has never been truer. No culture, no perks, and (next to) no amount of stock options can compel someone to follow a bad leader. A great leader is the glue that holds a team together.

Think about just how rare it is to find someone who combines vision, business acumen, and the ability to inspire others. But that is exactly what a sales development leader needs to possess. In the final part of this book, we'll focus on *day-to-day* leadership. We'll cover six key considerations:

1. Choosing the right captain
2. Equipping with a toolkit
3. Setting appropriate quotas
4. Architecting core processes
5. Using metrics to drive what matters
6. Implementing enablement technologies

These are the pillars of day-to-day leadership. Before we jump into these topics, let's turn our attention to a common question: *what exactly do leadership titles mean?*

Levels of Leadership

To set the stage, let me share my take on the levels of sales development leadership (see figure 30.1).

DIRECTOR	MANAGER	TEAM LEAD
THE VISIONARY AND GENERAL	THE COACH, WARDEN, AND THERAPIST	THE PLAYER COACH
Designs strategy	Optimizes execution	Executes process
Builds the ideal rep profile	Hires the ideal rep profile	Is the ideal rep profile
Seat at the executive table	Fantastic people motivator	Management-track potential
Great Strategist	**Great Coach**	**Great Role Model**

Figure 30.1 – Levels of leadership explained

I tend to think of it this way: managers *manage*, directors *direct*, and team leads . . . well, I'll share my opinion of that role a bit later. The level of your sales development leader isn't just about *title* or *compensation*. It's about the part you expect that individual to play in the team's success.

Director Level

Here's my rule of thumb: if your group is brand new (or evolving rapidly), you likely haven't yet 100 percent nailed down what repeatable and scalable success looks like. In that case, you need a director. You need someone who has created processes from scratch, knows when things are going awry, and (more importantly) has the skills to fix things.

Hiring an inexperienced leader (meaning someone in an SDR role and looking to move up) to do director-level work is a huge mistake. There's a time and a place for on-the-job learning, but it isn't when captaining a ship through a storm.

When you're building your team, it is all about experimentation. What's the right model? What process, messaging, and cadence work best? What are our ideal prospect types and qualification criteria? A *director* is someone who can interpret results and make course corrections—someone with experience who can take the overall goals delivered by the executive team and drive results. Directors have been here before. They've taken their lumps and are armed with the knowledge and experience that lets them hit the ground running.

Not sure of how to differentiate when you are in the heat of the hiring battle? Let me see if I can paint you a picture. One of my clients was interviewing for a director of sales development. His process included asking candidates to develop a 30-60-90-day plan—a fairly standard request for a hire at this level. One candidate, Ellie, didn't just go away and create it. She asked the hiring chief revenue officer (CRO) the following:

> In our second interview, you mentioned your 3-year plan. Can you share what has been communicated to the management team and the reps?
>
> Over the last 3-4 quarters, what challenges have been identified and what has been done to remove those obstacles?
>
> What career path/succession planning is outlined or implied at time of hire for the reps and managers?
>
> Please provide a review of current compensation model, implementation date and percent of reps exceeding, meeting and not meeting goal. Also, in your opinion, would a SDR be able to explain to their peer in less than 5 minutes how they get paid?

She asked damn good questions and demonstrated *director-level thinking.*

Manager Level

Once you've locked in on the strategy, built solid processes, and have metrics down, you're ready for a *manager.* Do a quick search on LinkedIn, and you'll find dozens of job descriptions for "sales development manager."

They all share these basic skillset requirements:

▶ Manage team to goals, objectives, and quota achievement

▶ Ongoing hiring, training, and coaching of reps

▶ Great communication and time management skills

▶ Provide detailed, weekly reporting

▶ Identify and make recommendations for improvement in the areas of process and productivity

These are table stakes when we're looking for a manager. If you're looking for a truly stand-out front-line manager, you need to search for attributes that aren't readily found by scanning résumés. To my mind, there are three key attributes:

1. **SKILL FOR SPOTTING TALENT:** Hiring reps in this competitive environment will be one of this person's greatest challenges. You need to hire a leader who, above all else, has the ability to spot great talent. In all likelihood, you're going to be hiring reps fresh out of college (or at a minimum early in their careers). Their résumés aren't going to tell the entire tale. Your leader has to be able to quickly figure out who will be able to do the job *tomorrow* (and be able to grow into the next role two levels up). Hiring for potential is no easy task, but finding a person who has the skill to identify potential is a huge win.

2. **HIGH MOTIVATIONAL ENERGY:** I don't know any other way to say this. Motivating a sales development team on a day-to-day basis is exhausting. Many reps are young and fairly inexperienced, and they suffer massive rejection daily. Your leader has to be able to keep the "happy" boat afloat. He or she has to have the endurance and the attitude to come to work every day and re-energize the team. Managers have to invest in engaging with reps, helping them see the bigger picture of how they fit into the corporate vision and reinforcing their value to the organization. That, combined with all

their other duties, makes motivational energy a must-have.

3. **ABILITY TO SIT AT THE TABLE:** A trend I am starting to notice is having sales development report directly to a C-level title (as do the leaders of sales and marketing). You should look for a candidate's ability to take a seat at the executive table (either now or in the future).

Team Lead Level

This brings us to our third and final level of leadership: *the team lead.* A team lead is a blended position—part day-to-day manager and part individual contributor with a personal quota. Let me be blunt: I'm not a fan of the team lead role (both in idea and in execution). Hiring an individual contributor with one foot in management and one foot as a rep can be a recipe for failure. If you've identified someone with the potential to be a fabulous leader, promote him or her. Asking someone to have one foot in the SDR world and one in the management realm is unfair and counterproductive.

Despite my vigorous objections, I know that some companies will head down this path. For those that do, here are three recommendations:

1. **GO SLOWLY:** We all know that there are no guarantees in hiring. Recall my earlier point about the 50 percent success rate for sales development hires? For a team lead, you want someone who will be an above-average *motivator and coach* as well as achieving his or her individual quota. If the team lead isn't able to do both and you have to let him or her go, now you're down a rep and your team is down a front-line manager. Not a great outcome.

2. **SET REALISTIC TIMEFRAMES:** Be direct about the realities of the role. What has to happen before the team lead can be promoted to full manager? What is your timeframe for transition? The worst-case scenario is your team lead thinking *months* and you thinking *quarters* for a promotion to full management timeframe.

3. **ASSIGN A FAIR QUOTA:** Let's say you expect your team leads to manage three reps at about 30 percent of their time. *How much quota relief should that give them*? My rule of thumb is to take the estimate for "time spent managing," add 20 percentage points, and reduce their quota by that amount. So if we suspect 30 percent spent on management, we should budget for a 50 percent reduction in quota. If you aren't willing to allow for that much quota relief, I strongly suggest you reconsider the role.

If you're a senior executive with other responsibilities, do yourself a favor and invest in hiring the level of leader you need. This is not the time to go cheap. Building a team from the ground up, including all the testing, experimentation, and changes it will require, is not something you want on your plate. Hand it over to someone who has the know-how and the passion for it. You won't regret the decision.

Promoting from Within

Here's a joke that has been around forever: What happens when you promote your top rep to manager? You lose your best producer and gain your worst leader.

To keep yourself honest, consider creating a first-line manager candidate profile. Jot down the skills and qualities you are most looking for in your first-line leader. Once, you have them down, reflect on which are *Must-Haves* (MHs) and which are *Nice-to-Haves* (NHs).

Let me try to frame this for you differently. You aren't just promoting your best rep as thanks for a job well done; you're evaluating him or her for an entirely different role requiring an entirely different skillset. The key is to be objective about what you're looking for and not view any candidate through rose-colored glasses. Your list might end up looking something like figure 30.2.

Creating a profile gives you a way to objectively evaluate both internal and external candidates based on what is *really* important.

	MUST-HAVE NICE-TO-HAVE OTHER
BUSINESS ACUMEN	
OPTIMISTIC	
ABILITY TO INSTIGATE CHANGE	
STUDENT OF THE GAME	
LEADERSHIP SKILLS AND MENTALITY	
PRODUCT, SOLUTION, MARKET KNOWLEDGE	
HISTORY OF SPOTTING GREAT CANDIDATES	
ENJOYS COACHING AND DEVELOPING	
OFFERS CONSTRUCTIVE CRITICISM	
BEEN SEEN BY PEERS AS A CAPTAIN (FORMALLY OR INFORMALLY)	
TAKES ON "EXTRA CREDIT" AND DELIVERS	

Figure 30.2 – Sample first-line manager candidate profile

Over my career, many of the best leaders I've worked with have made their way up from individual contributor roles. And many of the best reps I know have tried managing before realizing it wasn't for them. With internal candidates, you already know the following:

► Their work ethic and communication style

► The nature of their relationship with the team

► Their knowledge of market, buyers, product, and competition

► Their ability to navigate your internal systems and processes

► How well they are able to get things done in your organization

You can't underestimate the value of these factors. They will dramatically reduce the new manager's ramp time and significantly lighten the load on you. It all comes down to creating your *Must-Have* versus *Nice-to-Have* profile and being realistic about where each candidate falls against the ideal profile.

If you do promote from within, expect that a high degree of mentorship will be required. You'll have to assist your new manager as he or she navigates the transition from individual contributor to leader.

> *As an individual contributor, he or she was measured on one thing—achievement of quota. Now as a leader, he or she will be measured on ability to fill open slots, attrition rate, ability to motivate, and ability to effectively communicate both up and down. This is a very different landscape.*

Chris Snell, director of inside sales for Care.com, is someone who has successfully made the transition. Chris started his sales career as an SDR for an outsourced opportunity generation firm. He now leads a team of fifteen reps and two managers. Having once been given an opportunity himself, Chris is a firm believer in promoting from within. He shared that when looking for his next potential leader, a lack of prior management experience isn't a deal breaker. "I look for whether or not the rest of the team sees an individual as a leader. I want someone who's respected by their peers— someone who my reps go to when they have questions about selling, about our products, or about how to use the CRM. Those are the folks I'm looking at."

I think Chris summed it up beautifully. When promoting from within, the respect of the team is more important than a history of being a top rep. If you find someone who has both, put him or her on your shortlist. You also need to commit to being a mentor. I understand that a manager should be taking things off of your plate. But the candidate and the entire team need you to invest in making this person successful. The most important thing to remember is that the decision doesn't affect just you and the candidate. It affects your entire team.

CHAPTER 31

EQUIP THE TEAM

IF EVERY REP targeted your best prospects, told your best story, and ran your best process, how would that affect pipeline and revenue?

The reality for most teams is that one rep is the best at *choosing* prospects, another at *messaging*, and another still at *qualification*. But there isn't a single place where all that tribal knowledge and piecemeal excellence is collected and shared. Enter the sales development toolkit.

Your toolkit will give each and every rep the tools, tactics, and messaging to prospect like your best performers do. (These are often referred to as "binders," "playbooks," "handbooks," etc. For simplicity, I'll use toolkit.)A toolkit is the fastest way to get to repeatable and scalable sales development success. There shouldn't be any secret to your sales team's success. It should be spelled out in black and white.

Think about all the pieces you've included in onboarding new hires. If you're like most companies, all of that information is scattered across PowerPoints, PDFs, videos, Word documents, and ideas you've white boarded but never written down. Your SDR toolkit will take all that information and present it in a format that is concise, specific, visual, and actionable. In the toolkit, you'll ensure that

▶ A consistent message is being delivered

▶ What's working is being shared

▶ New hires ramp quickly

► Struggling reps have a map for what great "looks like"

► Reps are enabled, not left to hunt intranets, drives, and wikis

Kris Semb is responsible for worldwide sales development at IBM (which they call lead development). Just a decade ago, he was an SDR himself. In that short time, he worked his way up to manager, director, and then worldwide leader of more than five hundred reps. I asked Kris to share his philosophy on sales development toolkits. "The front lines of a sales organization have to be ready for just about anything. It's tremendously important for SDRs to rapidly find what they need to do their jobs. Over the years, I've found that an effective toolkit becomes a 'bible' of sorts. It's like the difference between manually combing through notes in a large notebook versus using Google to get ready, be ready, and find information on the fly."

As Kris suggests, a toolkit is a living and evolving document that's purpose built to make SDRs more effective. It's an integral part of your onboarding process as well as the gold standard your managers will coach against. Finally, it's one hell of a recruiting tool.

In this highly competitive market, wouldn't it be great to show a candidate your SDR toolkit and say, "Here is the roadmap for how the team executes. I look forward to you joining us and helping us to evolve this tool for future reps"?

Trust me, every hiring manager is claiming fantastic onboarding, training, and coaching. Show (don't tell), and you'll stand out from all the other companies you're competing with for talent.

Building a Toolkit

My team and I have built somewhere around one hundred sales development toolkits for clients. There are three things that are universally true:

1. The project is a lot of work (think months, not days).

2. There's no "I" in toolkit (well *technically* there is, but it still takes a

village).

3. Each company's toolkit is somewhat unique, but there is a *blueprint.*

There are many reasons leaders skip building a toolkit. Primary among them is a lack of time, followed closely by getting buy-in from senior leadership around what it takes to make this project a reality. "You should begin by identifying a problem that stems from the lack of a toolkit," shared Ralph Barsi, Senior Director, Global Demand Center at ServiceNow. "You can then go to senior leaders and say that we have a lot of new hires coming onboard because we are growing like crazy. We also have great tribal knowledge residing in our tenured reps. If we had a toolkit to reinforce the way our best reps are being successful, ramp time would be expedited and total productivity raised."

Ralph makes a pretty compelling case to take up with senior leaders. Even if you are the mythical triple-threat "great writer" + "sales enabler" + "sales manager" (*a wrenableger?*), you still need buy-in to devote the appropriate time and attention to building a toolkit. Also, you're going to need help.

Remember the cross-functional team we pulled together to build outbound messaging back in part 5? The best, fastest, and most painless way to build your SDR toolkit is to continue down that path. It is easy to get overwhelmed when you consider sitting alone in your office, staring at a blank page, and typing up a toolkit. Remember, you don't have to build it all at once, and you shouldn't try to do it alone. In working with clients, my team and I have a process that involves the following:

▶ Wide-participation web surveys

▶ Limited-participation interviews

▶ A thorough review of existing sales collateral

▶ Several half-day workshops

▶ An assigned editor process

▶ Team rollout and exercises

► A "best practices" audio library

► Future-proofing through regular revision and evolution

Ralph added, "You need a champion to create a bubble around you while you work on this. If this is a priority, you need to buckle down and move other stuff back onto the shelf." In a lot of organizations, that's just not realistic and you need to bring in outside help. The cruel irony of sales development is that *the moment* your group begins firing on all cylinders and you ramp up hiring (a huge time commitment in itself) is *exactly when* an SDR toolkit is needed most (yet another huge time commitment).

To help you along the way, I want to share the key sections of any SDR toolkit. Below, you'll find the blueprint I use with my clients. You are more than welcome to follow this flow in your toolkit (you can also see a sample table of contents at http://sdrbook.io/SAMPLETOC).

Section 1: Understand/Target

I can't reiterate strongly enough how critical it is that you teach your reps about your prospects and market before you teach them about your product. *Them before us* should be your mantra. In this section, you should include pieces such as a visual representation of your ideal customer profile, your "with us/without us" vision, and a cheat sheet for value propositions aligned to prospect personas. This section is all about understanding your prospects and using language that will resonate with them. It is the foundation for how your SDR team will communicate with your buyers in their conversations as well as in voicemail and email.

Section 2: Strategize/Plan

In this section of the toolkit, you will detail your processes for inbound lead qualification and/or outbound prospecting. Here is where you'll share a framework for effective pre-call planning: what information should reps capture, where do they put it for speedy future reference, and how do they use it in messaging?

Also, you'll map out your qualification criteria and sample questions. As you'll remember from part 1, that might be *"right profile, right person, right pain,"* "PACT: *Pain, Authority, Consequence,"* and *"Target Profile,"* or in certain rare cases BANT. Finally, you should define and document the entire process of scheduling, passing, and executing the meeting and/or the passing of a qualified opportunity to an account executive.

Section 3: Contact

In this section, you'll detail your multi-touch cadence and multimedia approach. You might have several cadences based on lead source, lead score, inbound versus outbound, etc. Knowing that each buyer type requires its own story, you'll lay out messaging themes by persona.

Here is where you should lay out those stories and tie them into your cadence and media strategy. For example, say you sell an applicant-tracking software system. You might sell to both staffing agencies and in-house hiring managers. Obviously, you wouldn't message to both the same way. Further, even within a company, you might target the VP of human resources, the director of recruiting, and the IT (information technology) director. For each of these, you'll want to provide a visual representation of how the story flows and how each touch your team delivers tells a different chapter of the story.

Section 4: Message

In previous sections of the toolkit, you've shared your "with us/without us" vision and value propositions by prospect persona. In this section, you want to give the team a framework for how to take all those things and create messaging that resonates.

You should include messaging samples as well as a framework for customizing and creating new emails and voicemails. The best way to illustrate this for the team is to take one of your prospect types and create the entire messaging story or cadence you will be executing. By creating a sample of the voicemails and emails this prospect will receive, you are providing a roadmap for the team to create their other prospect stories.

You'll also want to include customer stories. Teach the team to create and present them in a phone-ready format vs. a case study format (think *actionable sound bites*).

Section 5: Overcome

This section contains the ammunition your team needs to address common prospect objections as well as ready responses for the competition. You want to identify your most common objections and develop the responses you want your team to use. You want to share a framework to knock out objections but not knock the buyer. The same holds true for competitive situations. You'll want to create battle cards that allow your reps to knock out, but not knock, competitors.

Section 6: Execute

This is the final section in your toolkit. Here is where all the detail goes regarding how to leverage the technologies at the reps' disposal, what a perfect day looks like, how to effectively use the toolkit, you name it. Anything that relates to the tactical execution of the job will reside here. You'll also want to share baseline metrics (and expectations) that tell the story of how activity leads to results.

So there you have it. As I said earlier, each company's toolkit is slightly different and takes on the personality of the team itself. But this blueprint should serve as a good guide. There are a lot of other pieces that my team and I add to SDR toolkits for our clients (visuals, integrated video/audio, inspirational quotes, CRM integration, certifications), and they are important. But they are additive (not a replacement) for the sections outlined here. Give your group this roadmap to success. I've never met a sales development leader who regretted making this investment.

CHAPTER 32

SET APPROPRIATE QUOTAS

STATUS CHECK. Over the last few chapters, I've covered two of the six key considerations for leadership. Time for number three: *quotas*. Let me ask you, how do you know if you've set quotas appropriately?

Let's say it's the final week of December. You're looking back at your team's results this year. Which of the following is better, in your view?

OPTION 1: The team goal is made, 10% of reps hit quota, 90% miss
OPTION 2: The team goal is made, 90% of reps hit quota, 10% miss
OPTION 3: The team goal is made, 65% of reps hit quota, 35% miss

Almost no one would choose option one—although it is the cheapest option in terms of incentive compensation. Many would choose option two, the most expensive option. But for me, option three is the fingerprint of a well-set quota.

Before you object that one-third of reps missing quota is horrible, hear me out. When it comes to right-sizing quotas, everyone is looking for a magic formula that keeps the CEO, the CFO, the board, the leader, and the reps happy. Much like the unicorn, it just does not exist.

Setting fair quotas is about balancing interests—specifically:

▶ **CFO**: Cost of sales
▶ **CEO**: Productivity

► **Leader**: Team morale and retention

► **Reps**: Earnings potential and culture/climate

The first step in setting quotas is to admit that *quota* is a line in the sand, not the only marker of a good rep. I don't believe that *hitting quota* separates a good rep from a lousy one.

Think about it. Do you really believe that a rep who ends the year at 101 percent of goal is qualitatively better than one at 99 percent? I know I don't. That's a rounding error, not a marker of virtue or vice. The question we are left with is *how many reps should we expect to hit quota?*

Since 2007, the average percentage of reps at/above quota (in my research) has bounced between 63 percent and 74 percent. That feels about right to me. I know from analyzing more than eighty sales development teams that a group ending the year with 65 percent of reps at quota is fairly representative of the norm (http://sdrbook.io/SDRGRADER).

Quota Considerations

Okay. Now that we've agreed on what quota should actually mean (the level of performance that roughly 65 percent of reps will meet or exceed), we can turn our attention to quota setting. In figure 32.1, I've shared average quota benchmarks from my latest SDR Metrics research (http://sdrbook.io/SDRCOMP).

	INTRODUCTORY APPOINTMENTS	QUALIFIED OPPORTUNITIES
"PASSED" QUOTA	21	13

Figure 32.1 – Quota benchmarks by model

These numbers are averages, and (not surprisingly) actual quotas range widely. Unfortunately, companies sell into complex markets, not neat and tidy theoretical models. Here are two examples that show you the disparity.

Company A has an average selling price (ASP) of $115K.Quota for its outbound reps was just two qualified opportunities per month. Compare that to Company B, with an ASP of $5K. The quota for its inbound reps was forty-four introductory meetings per month. To give you a sense of what's at play, here are four variables you should take into consideration:

1. **ACTIVITY FOCUS:** Is your team qualifying inbound leads or conducting outbound prospecting? If inbound, how many leads will marketing generate? What is your historical conversion rate from *lead* to *SDR qualified*? If outbound, how well recognized is your brand in the market? This may seem like a strange question, but it matters. When your prospects hear your company name, does it make them more or less likely to take the call?

2. **MODEL:** Are you closing on interest? Or qualifying for need? Closing on an introductory meeting is much easier than fully qualifying an opportunity. As we discussed in part 1, you've already made the decision as to which model to implement. Obviously, you can't mix and match model and quota assumptions (e.g., require high-qualification and use low-qualification benchmarks).

3. **SIZE OF ACCOUNTS:** What size of company and what level within an organization are you targeting? Scheduling a call with the director of sales operations at a $20M software company and the director of sales operations at LinkedIn are two very different animals—even if an SDR is trying to introduce the exact same product or service. Similarly, it is much easier to reach the SVP of marketing at a $50M manufacturer than a marketing director of Amazon.com.

4. **MARKET MATURITY:** Are you selling into a mature market (where the need is understood) or immature (where the concept itself is new)? Just this week, I received an email from a rep at an electronic signature technology company. She asked about my availability to discuss our "esignature needs." The fact that I knew she meant *the sharing, tracking, signing, and storing of documents*

from any device means that the esignature is mature. The rep was able to use shorthand to orient me to what she was asking. If you're selling something that is not yet mainstream, your reps are going to have to work harder to hook those buyers. That needs to translate to lower quotas.

There is no way around it. Setting quotas is tough work. You can use the meeting setting (21) and qualified opportunity (13) numbers as benchmarks. Adjust up or down based on the four factors I've highlighted. Whether or not making quota is an achievable goal sets the tone for your culture. Make it attainable, and you'll have a group of competitive reps with a positive attitude. Make it too much of a stretch, and you'll have miserable reps and a high attrition rate.

You should also make use of ramped quotas for new reps. Let's say you determined that quota will be twelve qualified opportunities per rep per month. A ramp-up plan might look like this (see figure 32.2):

	MONTH 1	MONTH 2	MONTH 3	MONTH 4
NEW SDR RAMP	4	7	10	12

Figure 32.2 – Sample four-month ramping quota

Pipeline Expectation

The overwhelming majority of companies do not source 100 percent of sales pipeline from sales development. Based on my research, on average, 49 percent of company revenues are sourced by sales development groups. This is a number I've been tracking since 2009, and it has remained remarkably consistent. As you might expect, the smaller the company, the larger the share of revenue sourced by sales development (see figure 32.3).

It is tempting to build headcount assumptions from the ground up. And you should feel free to do so. But, again, keep in mind that V-E-R-Y few companies source 100 percent of pipeline from sales development. Your team, your account executives, and your CEO need to understand this fact and plan accordingly.

COMPANY REVENUE	% OF TOTAL REVENUE SOURCED BY SALES DEVELOPMENT
<$5M	61%
$5–19M	62%
$20–99M	53%
$100–249M	49%
$250M+	40%

Figure 32.3– SDR-sourced pipeline by company revenue

CHAPTER 33

BUILD YOUR PROCESS

I DISCUSSED THE IMPORTANCE of effective process with Nick Hedges, the CEO of Velocify who in part 3 shared his approach for screening for passion. Nick and I agreed that a mindset of hiring reps straight out of college, feeding them leads, and leaving them to figure out the rest needs to be weeded out. Nick shared that, in his research, "high-performing organizations are twice as likely as underperforming ones to be process-driven."

Great process is the foundation for repeatable, scalable success. Our reps bring passion, a competitive spirit, and curiosity to their jobs every day. It is up to us, as leaders, to engineer processes that channel their drive and maximize the return on effort.

To my mind, the four processes that sales development leaders should obsess over are the following:

- ▶ Cadence and media
- ▶ Speed-to-contact
- ▶ Account-centric prospecting
- ▶ The SDR-to-account executive handoff

I covered cadence and media in great detail in part 5. In this chapter and the next, I'll turn my attention to the remaining three.

Speed-to-Contact

A great deal of research has been published on the need for an extremely short timeframe between a prospect hitting "submit" on a web form and your rep placing the first outbound call. In InsideSales.com's *Lead Response Management Study*, the researchers found the following:

▶ Reps are ten times more likely to "contact" a lead if they call within the first hour of its creation.

▶ Reps are six times more likely to "qualify" a lead if they call within the first hour of its creation.

Those are pretty stark findings. But I must admit that I'm a bit conflicted on this topic. I can see how critical immediate response is in the business-to-consumer space, but I'm a bit of a skeptic as it relates to business-to-business. Let me paint you a picture.

Imagine your check engine light comes on. You make it to the office, pull up your local dealership's website, and fill out a "service request" form. You wait ten minutes and nothing. Another hour passes, still nothing. After two more hours, you still hear nothing. *What would you do next?* If you're like most people, you'd take your car elsewhere. Immediate response matters here.

So now let's transition to the business world. If a prospect visits your website and fills out a "Contact Us" form, it goes without saying that immediate response is required. But what if prospects download an e-book or register for a webinar? *What's the appropriate response time for them?*

My view is skewed by how I want to be treated. Here's a recent example. I signed up for a trial of a new software-as-a-service (SaaS) product the other day. I had *just* hit "register" on the company's website, and, before I even had the chance to log in, my phone rang with a call from an SDR. I have to admit I was impressed that the company takes leads so seriously, but at that point the only conversation the SDR was prepared to have was "I saw you signed up for a trial. How's it going so far?"

That's just plain silly. There has to be a middle path. As you think through the speed of your lead response, keep these two ideas in mind:

Rule 1: Not all leads are created equally.

Every lead doesn't necessarily deserve an equal application of resources. Of everyone who submits a form on your website, what percentage are Bread & Butter accounts? What percentage are Dead Ends? If you commit your reps to calling every lead within five minutes, marketing has to do an above-average job of scrubbing out non-ideal customer profile accounts. You can't allow just anyone with a pulse and the ability to hit "submit" to drive your team's activity.

Next, you have to think about what kind of prospect activity warrants immediate response. At Hubspot's recent *Inbound* conference, I asked an audience of roughly three hundred attendees how they defined an inbound lead. Was it:

- ▶ Only those who filled out a "contact me" or "request a demo" form?
  -or-
- ▶ Anyone who responded to any marketing campaign?

Resoundingly, the answer was the latter. For the majority of marketers, an "inbound lead" is defined as anyone who responds to your marketing outreach. If you commit your reps to calling every lead within five minutes, some prospects will be ready to schedule a call. But some will, for example, have registered for a future webinar or downloaded a whitepaper to read later. If you reach them live, what value will your reps have to offer?

There is a time and a place for speed-to-contact. For most companies, that isn't 100 percent of your inbound leads. You want to focus immediate response on a highly targeted subset of your leads who want (and warrant) that kind of attention.

Rule 2: Speed-to-lead requires pre-set plays.

Your reps don't have time to personalize a message when responding immediately. They have to have a pre-set *reason to call* ready to go. Calling quickly means your reps lack any time to conduct pre-call planning. But they need a better reason to call than "I saw that you downloaded something. How can I help you?" Let's say your product or service generally solves three big challenges. If you commit your reps to calling every lead within five minutes, you must enable them to (very quickly) link some attribute of a given lead with one of your three big benefits.

Your pre-set plays might resemble the following:

	RETENTION	PRODUCTIVITY	METRICS
VP OF SALES PERSONA	Impact of attrition on making the number	How high-growth companies enable their teams	Spot and address pipeline blind spots
SALES MANAGER PERSONA	Tactics for improving retention	Quick fixes for common hurdles	Using metrics in day-to-day coaching

Figure 33.1 – Sample pre-set plays

So if a rep were to receive a lead of a sales manager downloading a metrics report, the rep would know that he or she should lead with *using metrics in day-to-day coaching*. Or should an SVP of sales register for a webinar on productivity, the rep would lead with *how high-growth companies enable their teams*. This approach isn't perfect, but it is miles and miles beyond what most sales development groups are doing today.

Speed Limits

To help you think through where and when to deploy immediate response, consider a continuum. On one end, you have an inbound call to the sales line—the holy grail of inbound leads. Obviously, you don't want that prospect going to voicemail and waiting a day for a return call. On the opposite end, you have a new subscriber to your company's blog. Do you think the prospect (and the chance of passing him or her as a lead) is improved by immediate response? Probably not.

If you were to map out all your lead sources on a continuum of *immediate* response to *no* response, it might look something like this:

IMMEDIATE RESPONSE

Inbound sales call

"Contact Us" form

Demo request

New free trial

Stopped by booth at tradeshow

Attended a webinar

Downloaded e-book

Registered for webinar

Attended a tradeshow

Subscribed to blog

Followed the company on Twitter

NO RESPONSE

As you think through lead response time, let a well-thought-out strategy dictate your process, not a stopwatch. Let's turn our attention to the third process.

Account-Centric Prospecting

Sales leaders will often ask me, "Trish, what's the number one mistake you see sales development teams make?" You have heard me say it before, but my response remains the same: *they're processing leads—not prospecting for opportunities.* Here's what I mean.

Let's say your company sells animated video production services. (You know, the two- or three-minute animated "explainer" videos you see all over the web.) You've done great work on ideal customer profile and key prospect personas. They are:

► Software and professional services companies with under $25M in revenues

► VP/director of marketing or demand generation

Say a lead comes in for a company within that sweet spot, but the title is "senior marketing manager." A rep is assigned, and he or she is off to the races putting the contact through the process. *But what happens if the rep gets no response to the outreach?*

In most organizations, the story ends there. The rep would complete the process, mark the lead as "no contact," and let marketing take ownership to nurture. I call that approach *lead-centric processing.* A lead came in, got "processed" along the lead qualification conveyor belt, and was shot out the other end. But there's a better way.

When a (lower-level) contact takes some action, yes, your reps should follow up. Then, either at the same time or subsequently, they should reach out to a higher-level contact too.

In our example above, the inbound senior marketing manager lead should be thought of as an arrow to opportunity. That lead is a trigger event pointing you to that company. Something caused that person to raise his or her hand. Something is either currently underway or on the lead's radar screen. Processing the lead as a "one and done" isn't enough. Your reps should reach out to the VP of marketing and reference the inbound activity. They should go outbound to all the key personas within that account. In short, they should be prospecting for opportunity.

My advice is to coach your reps on a two-no's rule. An account shouldn't be marked "no contact" until at least two prospects have said no (or not responded). Most often, this means the lead and the boss/leader of the functional area. The biggest pushback I receive on this advice is about bandwidth. Leaders and reps alike will object that they have to meet SLAs for lead response time. And that they can't be calling prospects who aren't on their "list." I'm sure you'd agree that sales development should be in the business of building pipeline, not (only) satisfying SLAs. This requires a shift in mindset. But it is hugely important.

As you build your processes, remember: processing leads, no!— prospecting for opportunities, yes!

Now we are left with our fourth and final process: *the SDR-to-account executive handoff.* This is an area where I see significant pipeline leakage. You have built an amazing set of processes to get you to engagement with your buyer, and then you handoff the meeting or opportunity. If there is not an equally amazing set of processes on the account executive side of the house that executes in a consistent manner, you are in trouble. Remember, you can have the most productive SDR team on the planet, but if your handoff process is not rock solid and consistent, you will not achieve the conversion rates you need. That is the topic of our next chapter.

CHAPTER 34

PERFECT THE HANDOFF

ONE OF THE MOST DREADED ACRONYMS in all of sales is SLA (service level agreement). Account executives hate the notion of SLAs as just more middle-manager corporate speak. I prefer to couch it as rules of engagement for the handoff. Most are somewhat less allergic to that phrase.

Whether your reps are setting introductory meetings or passing qualified opportunities, they are likely calendaring time between the prospect and an assigned account executive. They go by many names: discovery calls, demos, briefings, or meetings. They can also be phone based or scheduled for face-to-face meetings. The most important thing is that your sales development team and your sales organization are aligned as to what a good "discovery call" looks like. This is an area where I regularly see pipeline leakage and effort being wasted.

The Agreement

Too many times, I've seen wasted effort (or worse yet, prospect frustration) when an SDR books a discovery call and the account executive either blows it off or does a half-assed job because he or she could tell "the prospect wasn't a good fit."

You'll want to remove most (if not all) subjectivity from the equation. When selecting your model and qualification criteria, everyone's opinions will already have been put on the table. Now you want to (briefly!) document that agreement. It might be as simple as the following (see figure 34.1):

RULES OF ENGAGEMENT	
MODEL	Introductory meetings
QUALIFICATION CRITERIA	Right profile, right person, and right pain
CALL OBJECTIVE	Meet subject matter expert for discovery call
ACCOUNT PROFILE	50–200 account executives Venture-backed/high-growth Decentralized sales team
CONTACT PROFILE	VP/dir. of sales (or sales ops)
ACCEPTANCE CRITERIA	Willing to see demo Access to power

Figure 34.1 – Sample SDR-AE handoff agreement

This is the first part of your agreement. All parties have to agree on what *good looks like*. Do this and dodge the bullet of subjective reasoning on what constitutes a valid introductory appointment.

Before the Call

Prior to the discovery call, your SDRs need to hand off the lead/opportunity to the account executive. Effective handoff requires calendaring a meeting, introducing all parties, communicating next steps, and setting an agenda for the discovery call. This is best handled by the SDR.

Once a discovery call has been agreed to, the SDR should immediately email both the prospect and the account executive. Here's a sample email:

Subject: Thanks for your time—next steps with SomeSoft

Dana,

Thank you again for your time. I'll be sending a calendar invite along shortly for April 12th at 12p.m.

To recap our conversation:

- You have 120 AEs (80 percent remote/field based).
- Accessing, updating, and reporting on the field's activity is a challenge.
- It is also affecting the ability to forecast accurately.
- Rich (SVP, sales) wants a fix in place by end of quarter.
- Solution must integrate with Salesforce.

Dana, please add and/or edit my recap where needed.

I've scheduled a call with Tom Sellers—direct dial: (617) 555.1212 and mobile: (857) 444.4545.

To ensure we're able to reach you in an emergency, would you mind sharing your mobile number as well?

Simple, but effective. The SDR has covered all bases and has communicated effectively with both the prospect and the account executive. This email chain is then captured inside of CRM for reference. A final step to the handoff is confirming the discovery call. This is the SDR's responsibility. The absolute best way to confirm a call is to text the prospect twenty-four hours in advance (obviously, you need his or her mobile number). Phone or email confirmations are fine, but there is always the risk of the prospect "missing" the confirmation. Most people—from a sixth grader to the CEO of a Fortune 500—never miss a text message.

During the Call

I am a firm believer in the SDR participating in the discovery call. There is no better training experience than live listening. The reps are able to hear how their account executive counterparts move a prospect through the sales process and (equally important) how prospects respond. You might object that this takes them off the phone. Yes, it does. Get over it. You should be thrilled that another member of your organization is assisting in developing the skills of your reps.

Assuming that you are onboard with SDRs participating in discovery calls, I suggest letting them kick the call off by making introductions. The SDR then moves into listening and learning mode. If at all possible, record the call (again, depending on call recording laws and/or asking for permission to record). Note taking isn't as effective as recording a sales call. The recording can be used for review purposes or training in the future.

This also frees up both parties to communicate over a backchannel during the call. If the SDR and AE are in the same room, they can mute the line. If they are not, they can use corporate instant messaging or (silenced!) text messaging.

At the end of the call, it is the account executive's responsibility to identify and confirm next steps: *Who is doing what in what timeframe? What did the prospect and account executive commit to?* Closing out a discovery call without a confirmed next step is just a waste, so have a process in place to make sure it does not happen and track those outcomes.

After the Call

Two things need to happen once the call has been completed. First, the SDR and the account executive should debrief immediately. They should discuss the following:

- ▶ How well did the call go?
- ▶ How could we have done better?
- ▶ Is this a real opportunity?
- ▶ If not, why not?

There is no better time for feedback and coaching on why the opportunity will (or won't) be accepted than the moments immediately following the call. Second, the account executives need to take ownership of the lead/create an opportunity in CRM. In reality, this likely won't happen immediately. But they need to do it within twenty-four hours. Even if the opportunity is at 0 percent, this process confirms acceptance by the account executive. Because SDRs will be measured (or compensated, promoted, etc.) on this metric, the loop needs to be closed. Because you have already established firm acceptance criteria, this should be relatively painless. Again, you want to remove all subjectivity from the process.

Future-Proofing

The particulars of the handoff process and really all the sales development processes work best when the team buys in. The best sales development groups are open and collaborative. They harness the best ideas, insights, and innovations—whether they come down from the leader or up from team members.

VMTurbo is one such organization. Natasha Sekkat, the sales leader who shared her strategy for hiring in groups in part 3, heads up sales development at VMTurbo. A challenge that many sales development leaders face is the diversity and quantity of projects on their plates. Natasha and one of her managers came up with an interesting strategy: give the SDRs themselves ownership to work on *special projects*. They constructed a white board where each project is represented by a magnetic green circle. (VMTurbo's logo has a green circle.) Each green circle lists the project, the originator, and the names of the contributors. The circles move from left to right as they progress and are completed.

Natasha shared, "This has been amazing. We're diversifying what the SDR role means. It isn't just pick up the phone and dial, dial, dial. It's also to come up with ways to help us build a better business. I've been amazed by the quality and creativity of my team's ideas. They're identifying and solving problems I didn't even know we had."

Natasha leads more than 150 reps and managers. That is a substantial group. While she has ultimate responsibility for the ideas, strategies, and processes of her group, imagine what tapping into the passion and enthusiasm of that pool of people could mean.

You can attract and recruit the best. You can motivate and compensate them to perform. But you can't compel them to be creative or to be problem solvers. You have to build an environment that encourages reps to "volunteer" their best ideas.

CHAPTER 35

MEASURE WHAT MATTERS

ONE OF THE BEAUTIFUL THINGS about sales development is that it's so measurable. One of the ugly things associated with sales development is that it is so measurable. As in all things, there is a balance between science and art in metrics for measuring success.

Yes, metrics are hugely important. But the biggest impact comes from understanding the difference between *the piles of data* and *the information and insights* that help make decisions and affect the performance of your team.

In this chapter, we're going to cover three major categories of metrics and how you can use them to improve performance.

In the fantastic book *Cracking the Sales Management Code*, Jason Jordan and Michelle Vazzana identified 306 metrics that leaders use to manage their teams. Shockingly, the authors found that only 17 percent of those metrics are able to be managed. While *Cracking the Sales Management Code* is focused on effectively managing an AE sales force, I'm confident the findings hold for sales development.

By asking "Can a manager manage this?" they were able to take all those metrics and put them into three categories:

> ▶ **RESULTS:** the outcomes that are incredibly important to the business but outside the control of sales management

► **OBJECTIVES:** areas that can be influenced by sales managers but still are outside their direct control

► **ACTIVITIES:** things that are under the direct control of the managers and as a result can be proactively managed by them

What the book's authors are highlighting is important. Say your CEO walks into your office and asks, "I noticed that Brian is still struggling. What are you working on with him?" You wouldn't reply, "No worries, I told him to improve the quantity and quality of the leads he's passing. He said he'd get it done by the end of this week." That is a terrible response. Remember: leaders can't directly manage (and reps can't directly control) *Results*. You have to peel back the onion and focus on *Objectives* and *Activities*.

There's also a big difference between being data *driven* and data *informed*. I'm 100 percent in the camp of using data to lead a team. I feel equally strongly that data shouldn't drive the manager; the manager should use data to drive decisions. Data is just a tool. A fool with a tool is still a fool. Consider this example.

Three Reps

Imagine you have three reps on an outbound team setting introductory appointments: Paul, Vicki, and Rory.

Paul excels at pre-calling planning. His messages are tight, relevant, and effective. But his total activity levels are well below the target. Vicki, on the other hand, is a dialing machine. She consistently tops the leaderboard for activity. Compare them to Rory, who splits the difference with activity levels somewhere between Paul and Vicki. If we just looked at total activity metric (dials + emails +other), Vicki is the "best" rep.

So should Paul and Rory be coached to be more like Vicki? It seems logical that if they were just to increase their activity levels to where Vicki is performing, they'll set more appointments. I can tell you from experience that that isn't quite how it works. Pressuring reps to go against their DNA can work for boosting an Activity metric, but it won't work for boosting Results.

That's why the third category of sales development metrics, Sales Objectives, is so important. Let's take a look at the team's number of "quality conversations" per week.

I define a quality conversation as any interaction where at least one piece of qualifying/disqualifying information is learned. (If you're looking for something less subjective, you could assume any call lasting longer than 120 seconds.)

	TOTAL WEEKLY ACTIVITIES	QUALITY CONVERSATIONS PER WEEK
PAUL	310	32
VICKI	520	38
RORY	400	46

Figure 35.1 – Three-rep comparison

Now a different picture begins to emerge. If you led this group, how would you coach each rep individually? Personally, I might discuss time spent on pre-call planning with Paul. There is a fine line between effective research and becoming a prospect's unauthorized biographer. Paul needs to do a little less *pre-call planning* and a little more *calling* to improve his conversation numbers. With Vicki, I might cover messaging. What is she saying in all those voicemails and emails? Her ratio of conversations per activity is way off. Perhaps a little more time spent on customization would improve the number of quality conversations. Or maybe she is calling prospects well past the point of diminishing returns and needs to limit her number of attempts.

I suspect you get my point.

Activities we can manage: *make more dials, try this in your messaging, make more dials during prime calling hours.* Reps can take that coaching and put it into place tomorrow. The number of quality conversations is an Objective. Managers can influence it, but reps can't head back to their desks and immediately deliver more quality conversations by the end of the day.

Prospects just stubbornly refuse to cooperate with our sales plans!

Avoid Abstraction

First, a quick disclaimer: *I'm going to avoid acronym speak.* The terms *Inquiry*, *MQL*, *SAL*, and *SQL* are used regularly in the sales and marketing universe. There's a pretty big problem though—they aren't being used consistently from company to company.

Yes, I know that MQL stands for "Marketing Qualified Lead" (duh!), but what does that *mean* exactly? In the last two months, I've worked with three companies with three different definitions. One considered MQLs any inbound lead. Another called any prospect targeted by an SDR an MQL. A third used MQL to describe introductory meetings set by the sales development team. Um . . . okay? Here's my advice:

> *Speak English. Don't use abstractions. If you're wondering what to call an SDR-sourced opportunity, don't call it a three-letter acronym that means nothing. Call it what it is: either an SDR-sourced opportunity or something else that means something to the team.*

I understand that senior executives often expect this type of language. But the problem is that not every company uses the same order. For one company, the waterfall flows: Marketing Qualified Lead -> Sales Accepted Lead -> Sales Qualified Lead. Another may order it Marketing Qualified Lead -> Sales Qualified Lead -> Sales Accepted Lead.

Helpful, no?

The next time you confront three-letter acronym benchmarks, remember to dig beneath the abstraction and get at what exactly each stage is trying to communicate. There's no point in wasting cycles trying to benchmark against mismatched metrics.

I've shared my suggestions in figure 35.2. What my terms lack in business school flair, they make up for in clarity. Feel free to use your own terms or even the dreaded three-letter acronyms. If you do pull metrics off the internet, just don't expect how they're being used is how you're using them internally.

	DEFINITION
SUSPECT	Inbound lead/inquiry generated by marketing
PROSPECT	Outbound target that meets the ideal customer profile
DISCOVERY CALL	A meeting/opportunity sourced by an SDR (Stage 0 pre-pipeline)
ACCEPTED OPPORTUNITY	An accepted SDR-sourced opportunity (Stage 1 pipeline)
WIN	Closed won business

Figure 35.2 – Non-abstract terms for metrics

Make sense? Okay, on to our metrics.

CHAPTER 36

MANAGE WITH MEANINGFUL METRICS

OUR FIRST CATEGORY focuses on activities. These are the metrics we use to not only measure individual rep performance, but improve upon it. The Activity metrics you'll want to measure include the following:

- ▶ Total activities per day
- ▶ Inbound lead response time
- ▶ Attempts per lead
- ▶ # of prospects per account

These are the metrics that leaders can manage and reps can control. I know there's a chorus that loves to crow that "activity is an outdated tactic and ratios and results are all that matter." I offer two responses.

First, telling reps, "Hit your number; I don't care how you get there," is great bravado and terrible management. Informing your reps that *x activities* will lead to *y outcomes* and drive *z results* is real leadership. Second, how exactly does one calculate ratios without measuring activity? Unless the fundamentals of math have changed—and I have been out of school a while— you need both the number of connects and the number of total activities to figure out a connect rate.

You'll also use Activity metrics to validate that your processes are being followed. Say you've built a seven-attempt cadence. You'll want to measure that it is being followed. For example, you might report on number of attempts for "no contact" leads (meaning prospects who were attempted but never reached). Similarly, if you're conducting account-centric prospecting, you'll want to measure the number of prospects attempted per lead.

Objectives

The next category of metrics deals with Objectives. These are the metrics you'll use to inspect, diagnose, and coach your reps. If you'll allow me to absolutely murder a line from Tolstoy (sorry Leo!): *no great rep is alike; each struggling rep is struggling in his or her own way.* The Objective metrics you'll want to measure include the following:

▶ # of connects/connect rate

▶ # of quality conversations/rate

▶ Email response rate

▶ "Bad data" rate

Connects and Quality Conversations

It is tempting to assume seventy activities means twelve connects, eight quality conversations, and one introductory meeting per day. While it seems nice and clear on paper, reality is much murkier. Not every dial has the objective of booking a meeting. Activities can be made to conduct research, identify direct-dial phone numbers, or collect other information within the organization. Also, it often takes more than one conversation to set an introductory meeting with a given prospect. And in some cases, it takes multiple conversations with multiple prospects to qualify an opportunity. These are all critical components of the sales development process.

I believe that *number of quality conversations* is one of the most important indicators of rep proficiency. Does a given rep have the ability to arouse curiosity and launch a conversation with a prospect? Or is the rep being shut down and kicked to the curb from the get-go? This is the type of metric you can use to diagnose and address with coaching.

Pete Gracey is CEO of QuotaFactory. We met him earlier when he shared how he screens for curiosity in interviews. Pete put it this way: "We use the 'connects' as a measure of data quality. Is the list good? Are we giving reps what they need to reach the right prospects? We use 'quality conversations' as a measure of rep skill."

A rep's number of quality conversations is a good indicator of effectiveness. Recall Paul, Vicki, and Rory, whom we met earlier. I've updated the table to include their connect metrics.

	TOTAL WEEKLY ACTIVITIES	QUALITY CONVERSATIONS PER WEEK	QUALITY CONVERSATION RATE
PAUL	310	32	10%
VICKI	520	38	7%
RORY	400	46	12%

Figure 36.1 – Three-rep comparison with rate

Using these metrics, we're able to see that Vicki's quality conversation rate is much lower than those of the others. We might work with her on how to open a call and have buyer-based conversations. We can also see that Paul's connect-to-quality conversation rate is strong, but we need to nudge his total activity level higher. This level of detail drives personalized, one-on-one coaching. That is the biggest value of Objective metrics.

Conversation Rates

Callback rates are a terrible annoyance to track. The numbers will invariably be less than staggering and require reps to log all return calls. I prefer to use conversation rate as a proxy. Say you have historically been calling HR directors. Now you're also calling sales VPs. How do those conversation rates compare? These metrics will give you a great idea of where your message is best resonating. You're looking for the message that creates forward momentum. Identify and share that message, and your group will have better outcomes.

Email Response Rates

You can also use email response rates as a proxy for messaging effectiveness. I prefer to use reply rates (there are several technologies that can supply this). Email open rates are less valuable (and notoriously unreliable). Assuming you can trust them, open rates will indicate subject line effectiveness. Many groups have experienced great results measuring and A/B testing subject lines.

With reply rates, you can be 100 percent confident that messages are being noticed and read. You have to correct for positive versus negative responses, but on the whole you'll have a good idea of which emails are working. Next, you and the team can take a longer look at your templates, assess which parts are working, and create new variants.

Bad Data/No Fit Rates

You'll want to measure the rates at which your reps are disqualifying leads for "bad data" or "bad fit." Data quality is neither sexy nor fun, but it is one of your best levers for more productivity—particularly with outbound sales development.

Think of it this way: every minute your reps spend figuring out whom to call or how to get at them is a minute they aren't spending talking to prospects.

You'll want to create a way to track bad data in your CRM and use that metric as a way to fight for the funds to invest in a data cleanup and append program. On the inbound SDR side of the house, we need to measure and monitor "no fit" rates. This isn't specifically about the performance of your team, but it is an important aspect to measure and share with marketing. Everyone needs to know which lead sources create the best leads (notice I didn't say the most leads). One hundred tradeshow leads (that may/may not fit your ideal customer profile) are worth less than twenty-five Bread & Butter leads. Get marketing on the same page with this metric. You've committed to meeting a Service Level Agreement for follow-up, and they should commit to meeting a Service Level Agreement for fit/no fit.

Results

This brings us to the final category of metrics: Results. You may recall from the previous chapter that Result metrics are "the outcomes that are incredibly important to the business but outside the control of sales management." These are the metrics you'll be reporting up to with senior leadership. The Result metrics you'll want to measure include the following:

- ▶ # of discovery calls
- ▶ # of discovery calls accepted as opportunities/acceptance rate
- ▶ Show/no-show rate (relevant for introductory meeting model)
- ▶ $ SDR-sourced pipeline
- ▶ $ SDR-sourced wins
- ▶ % of total pipeline sourced by SDRs
- ▶ $ won per account executive (relevant for new groups—e.g., pre-/post-SDR team)

Discovery Calls/Accepted Opportunities/Won Business

It goes without saying that these are the metrics that matter. These are the results the business cares about and how you'll likely be compensating your reps, and they will factor into micro-promotions. Earlier, I shared average quotas for "passed" introductory meetings or qualified opportunities. From that same research (http://sdrbook.io/SDRMETRICS), here are the average accepted numbers (meaning discovery calls that an account executive accepts into pipeline).

	INTRODUCTORY MEETINGS	QUALIFIED OPPORTUNITIES
PASSED	21	13
ACCEPTED	11	9
CONVERSION	52%	69%

Figure 36.2 – Average "passed" and "accepted" quotas

No doubt you noticed that qualified opportunities convert to accepted opportunities at a much higher rate. If they didn't, we'd probably begin to question the meaning of the word "qualified." In terms of acceptance rates, I prefer to see a range of 40 percent to 50 percent for introductory meetings and 65 percent to 75 percent for qualified opportunities.

You should be watching out for significant deviations above or below those thresholds. Too far above, and it might mean your sales team is just accepting anything—either because they are in dire need of at-bats or because they want their SDR partner to feel good. Too far below, and it might mean that the account executives are looking for better qualified opportunities (time to revisit that agreement) or that your SDRs aren't living up to their end of the agreement. Either way, you have some work to do to figure this out.

Show/No-Show Rate

If you are setting introductory meetings, the cruel truth is that no-shows are a reality. A no-show rate of 15 percent to 20 percent is normal. Any more than that and you should evaluate whether your reps are sparking curiosity or badgering prospects to accept meetings they don't ever plan on attending.

In the SalesHacker LinkedIn group, Robyn Lightner (business development team manager at Salsify) shared how she tracks the percentage of scheduled appointments that occur. Salsify calls this metric SUR, for "Show Up Rate": "You can't just punt the prospect over the wall to your AE and move on—you need to do everything you can to get it there and make sure she catches it. Our starting goal is 75 percent SUR, including reschedules that do wind up occurring. The SUR goal is a more positive way of approaching this part of the Service Level Agreement without having a 'clawback' for no-shows. Our reps need to maintain a trailing 90-day average of greater than 75 percent SUR in order to advance to the next tier in our promotion program."

Robyn's solution is a fantastic way to address this issue. As we discussed in part 4, our approach should be to promote on achievement, not tenure. Show rate is an important metric when considering career path and/or micro-promotions. Her strategy also reframes a negative (clawing back compensation) as a positive (exceed this and advance).

Sourced Pipeline and Won Business

Happily, we are light years away from having to justify the concept behind a sales development team. Having said that, we still must track contribution in terms of top of the funnel. Senior leadership will expect you to be ready with how much overall pipeline your group has sourced.

You'll also want to be ready with the percentage of total pipeline sourced. This metric is one of my favorites. This is the impact metric. What percentage of the overall pipeline was created by the SDR team? There is no right or wrong number here, as it is so heavily dependent on your business model.

High volume, heavy inbound, and/or transactional sales model, and the number is higher. More complex, bigger-ticket sales model, and the number is lower. Work with your executive team to put a line in the sand for what percentage needs to come from your SDR group, and then manage against it.

Examples: If the contribution number is higher than you anticipated and the members of the sales team are not hitting their goals, you probably need to evaluate whether they have become too dependent on the SDR team to fill their funnel. Conversely, if the contribution number is too low, you probably need to look at whether your original expectations were realistic or if your sales organization is rejecting opportunities too quickly.

Closed revenue via meetings/opportunities sourced: This is just basic math. You want the revenue generated to more than cover the expense of your SDR team. The "how much more" equation will depend on a variety of factors: maturation of the team, average deal size, inbound vs. outbound, etc.

Dashboard

Now that we've gathered metrics, I want to provide examples of how you might put them together in a dashboard. The best dashboards provide a single place to access near-real-time indicators of group performance. When building sales development dashboards, I keep three things in mind:

- ▶ Which metrics
- ▶ What timeframe
- ▶ For which audience

Over the years, I've seen and requested, usually from sales operations, a wide variety of dashboards. I've settled on a basic blueprint or group dashboard—this should be shared with the first-line manager as well as the team.

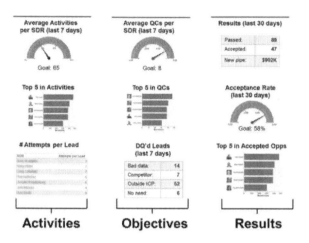

Figure 36.3– Sample SDR team dashboard

I like this dashboard because of its clarity. It clearly breaks out activities, objectives, and results in a manner that is easy to read and digest. My favorite metrics in this dashboard include the following:

▶ Attempts per lead
▶ Disqualified lead reasons
▶ Acceptance rate

There is much to be learned about overall team health from those data points.

CHAPTER 37

ENABLE WITH TECHNOLOGIES

ACCORDING TO RESEARCH FROM INSIDESALES.COM, business spending in the sales acceleration category in North America alone recently crossed $13B. That's billion with a "b." This brings to mind a well-worn quote from John Wanamaker: *"Half the money I spend on advertising is wasted; the trouble is I don't know which half."*

I saw on Twitter recently that, just within the last ten years, more than two thousand sales automation applications have been brought to market. Now, I'm sure half of those technologies are fantastic; I'm just not sure which half.

The technologies you implement for your team are critical. Great technology implemented well has the potential to accelerate excellence. The wrong technology, no matter how well implemented, has the potential to accelerate "suck." In this chapter, I'll share the key sales development technology stack and provide a framework for thinking about their impact.

There's a term for applications that accelerate effectiveness and are popular with reps: *tools*. There's also a term for highly popular applications that don't move the productivity needle one millimeter: *toys*. When I consider SDR acceleration technologies, I try to keep the following 2×2 grid in mind (see figure 37.1).

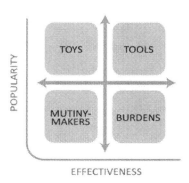

Figure 37.1 – SDR acceleration technology 2×2 grid

Our goals as sales development leaders (and acceleration technology buyers) are four-fold.

1. **ELIMINATE THE MUTINY-MAKERS:** If it isn't helping reps be more productive and they hate using it, rip it out. As an example, consider all the extra clicks, fields, and drop-downs in CRM that reps are required to fill out—but are never used by the business to make decisions. They key is to eliminate "prior management debt" (aka required fields from two sales VPs ago) to streamline the process.

2. **ALLEVIATE THE BURDENS:** Manual commission tracking would fall into this category. Let's face it: reps will always be tracking deals to make sure they get paid. But if they are building and reviewing Excel sheets line by line, that time is being wasted. A single system of record for commissions might give them the visibility they want without the wasted hours and effort.

3. **THIN THE TOYS:** Whether or not these technologies increase effectiveness, reps love them. You have to keep some of them around for morale. The key is to limit the amount of your technology budget that ends up in this quadrant.

4. **DOUBLE DOWN ON TOOLS:** This is true sales acceleration. These applications actually *increase* productivity, and you don't have

to bribe (or threaten) reps to adopt them. To my mind, automated dialers and email trackers (discussed in more detail below) are two shining examples.

The biggest differentiator between tools and toys is less "Does the product work?" and much more "Will it work here?" "So many technologies demo fantastically well," shared Nancy Nardin, founder of Smart Selling Tools. "But leaders have to ask, are we really going to use it? Do I have the support? Do I have the know-how? Do I have the time? Will my AE adopt it?" Those are the big issues you need to consider. Implementation and adoption are what separate the tools from the toys.

In the remainder of this chapter, I'm going to share the most important categories of tools that truly accelerate sales development. I'm not going to make specific vendor recommendations in any of them. You can use Google, Quora, LinkedIn, and G2Crowd to find plenty of suggestions. I'll also share caveats where I think a purchase in a given category makes more (or less) sense. And finally, I'm going to assume a baseline that includes a great headset, dual monitors, and a customer relationship management system (CRM) where the user experience has been customized for sales development. Let's get started.

Category 1: Account and Contact Data

Access to a database of accurate names, titles, email addresses, and direct-dial phone numbers is far from sexy. But that is the foundation of sales development success. For outbound teams, this is a must-have purchase. Executing outbound prospecting with a lousy list is like running uphill, in the mud, facing the wind, with a 70-lb.bag strapped to your back. Seriously. Steve Richard from ExecVision did an analysis for his team. He took a look at meetings set by six of his reps and found that for every 10 percentage point increase in the number of direct dials, his reps set roughly four more meetings. Steve (ever the comedian) had this to share: "Now, I'm no statistician, but I do know a straight line when I see it."

For inbound qualification teams, data matter too. Prospects will often mistakenly mis-enter their contact information (let's try to be generous and assume it is in error). Reps are then forced to hunt for better information or navigate a labyrinth of automated phone trees. If your reps are adding a second contact to their process for inbound leads (think calling the CMO when the marketing director comes inbound), we need to make that process easy for them.

Every moment your team spends trying to figure out *whom to call* and *how to reach them* is lost to actually engaging with prospects. Make an investment in building your database and keeping it fresh.

Category 2: Sales Intelligence

Time spent customizing messaging can easily grow out of control. Yes, reps need to conduct pre-call planning to personalize their messaging. But there's a tendency to research and customize well past the point of diminishing returns. Sales intelligence tools put high-value research points at your reps' fingertips. Many technologies integrate and sit right inside your CRM. This can include recent new events, mergers and acquisition, missed earnings, and new technologies in use.

For inbound groups, this can be a nice-to-have. If the winds are in your favor, you'll already know what campaigns prospects responded to, the pages they viewed on your website, and more. For outbound groups—and particularly those calling into large companies and popular titles (VP of sales, CIO, director of IT)—sales intelligence helps reps stand out from the crowd. Much as we discussed in chapter 25, pre-call planning takes good messaging and elevates it to great with one-to-one personalization.

One final point: don't underestimate what you can learn via social channels. It goes without saying that LinkedIn is the mothership, but your reps can learn a lot by following your buyers on other channels (Twitter, Quora, etc.). While it isn't likely that they will find a list of top initiatives this quarter with specific budget amounts, there is plenty that can be used to cut through the noise and get prospects to stop and listen.

Category 3: Dialing Platform

In figure 37.2, I've shared quality conversation metrics from the SDR Metrics research I've presented earlier (http://sdrbook.io/SDRMETRICS).

AVERAGE DIALS PER DAY	QUALITY CONVERSATIONS PER DAY
<39	4
40–59	6
60–79	7
80–99	9
100+	10

Figure 37.2 – Dials and quality conversations per day

Unsurprisingly, the use of automated dialers increases the number of average dials per day reps make. (I'd be worried if it didn't!) It also increases the number of quality conversations per day by nearly thirty percent. And that's what you're looking for.

There is significant value in simple features, such as click-to-dial and automated task creation, and advanced features, such as automatic call recordings and local presence. For those unfamiliar with local presence, when a rep places a call, the prospect sees a caller ID number that is local. For example, if I'm calling from Boston (617 area code) into Atlanta (404 area code), caller ID would show a 404 number.

I also consider the combination service-technology tools as part of this category. These technologies allow SDRs to load lists into a portal and multiple reps on the service provider side to do the dialing. Your reps don't have to punch in phone numbers, navigate phone trees, speak with gate keepers, etc. They sit on a bridge and wait for (BEEP!) an instant transfer when a live connection is made and a screen pop-up indicating who is on the other end of the line. Even with an average-quality list, these services can deliver five to eight connects *an hour*. That is a massive increase over the average of ten to twelve connects *per day*.

From my research, I know that fewer than half of sales development groups use dialing technology. That's a shame as reps who use these technologies love them. As we discussed above, high effectiveness plus high popularity is the definition of a sales acceleration *tool*.

Category 4: Email Platform

As I shared in part 5, I'm a believer (but not fanatic) in using email as part of effective sales development execution. There is a host of technologies that allow reps to view who is opening and clicking on their emails and when. These are the basic features of an email platform. Advanced features include the following:

▶ Send later—pre-schedule emails for future delivery

▶ Reminders—set tasks to follow up on important messages

▶ Templates—create, share, and report on which templates are getting the best reply rates

▶ Mail merge—send small personalized email campaigns

▶ Attachment analytics—see how engaged recipients are with content shared over email

▶ Insert calendar—plot available times within an email and simplify the process of agreeing on a time to meet

I want to highlight the impact of a few of these features. The ability to *insert calendar* vastly simplifies the meeting scheduling process. It reduces double bookings, eliminates annoying "calendar battleship," and generally reduces the headache of trying to agree on a time. *Send later* is an extremely useful time saver. Say your outbound prospecting cadence calls for reps to personalize messaging with pre-call planning (and I hope it does!). They do their homework and leave a prospect a voicemail as their first attempt. *Isn't now the best time to craft the email for their send attempt?* If your cadence has that email being sent after two days, reps can use send later to pre-schedule that email and save time on another round of pre-call planning. This single use case is a huge productivity booster and major time saver.

There is no silver bullet technology bundle for all that ails your sales development team. You know that. Spending money on toys, or tools for that matter, is a lot easier than working on strategy, recruitment, retention, or execution. But that hard work must happen first. You have to be rock solid on the other five elements before looking to technology to automate or accelerate.

Peggy Budnick, senior global director of inside sales at Apigee, shared this advice with me. "It's too easy to shift into more of a technology manager and less of a people leader. There's a whole industry cropping up around sales development. Sales operation teams are often measured on finding the newest and best mousetrap. They're constantly tapping you on the shoulder about a new tool. But automation can go too far."

There's a dreaded disease I'm seeing spread across sales development. It's called "WTF": *Wasted Technology Funds*. Don't catch it! When you think about investing to increase the productivity of your team, shun the mutiny makers, limit the toys, and double down on the tools.

PARTING THOUGHTS

EVERY DAY, I'm excited to get up, go to work, and talk to sales development practitioners like you. It's my goal to learn something new and interesting each day. No matter what it says on my business card, I'm the *chief sales development evangelist,* and it's absolutely the best job in the world. I hope you feel the same way about your role, too! Today's SDRs are future account executives. Current first-line managers are future directors. Executives like you are future chief revenue officers and founders/CEOs. Sales development is shaping the future of companies, industries, and economies.

What you do matters. You have the ability to influence not only the culture of your team, but also how your company is perceived by prospects. You have the chance to shape not only the career trajectory of dozens and dozens of reps, but also the growth path of your entire organization. For you personally, success with this team isn't just a stepping stone; it's a giant leap forward in your career.

You aren't just "running" sales development; *you're changing the world.*

If you're a sales development veteran, I know change is hard, and I appreciate the time you've taken to read these pages. Don't be afraid to experiment. Don't be afraid to push yourself and your team. I hope the six elements have given you plenty of food for thought.

If you are brand new to leading sales development, I'm so happy for you! What an exciting time to join the movement. I know you'll be a fantastic strategist, coach, and leader. As you think your way through the six elements, I hope this book will be your faithful companion and trusty guide.

Hopefully, this isn't the end of our conversation. I blog about sales development metrics and trends at http://blog.bridgegroupinc.com, my Twitter handle is @bridgegroupinc, and I run a sales development group on LinkedIn (http://sdrbook.io/LIGROUP).

I want to keep learning, too. I feature the best thinking from sales development practitioners on my blog. I hope you'll share your story. Don't hesitate to email me at trish@bridgegroupinc.com. I look forward to those conversations. According to a recent headline on Forbes.com, the biggest trend in sales today is this thing called sales development, and I couldn't agree more.

Here's to building repeatable pipeline. Here's to accelerating growth. And—most of all—here's to you.

ACKNOWLEDGMENTS

I lead a blessed life, both professionally and personally. For me, there is no barrier between the two—not being an entrepreneur was never an option. And for that, I thank my parents who taught me that the road to success is paved by those who dare to think outside the mainstream. Thank you Mom and Dad for never doubting and always encouraging.

I've never had a burning passion to be an author. But as I write these words, I can say in all honesty: this is one of my life's major accomplishments. Jill Konrath convinced me to write this book. Jill, you were right, I had to but never would have without your repeated kicks in the butt.

Matt Bertuzzi, I have no idea how to thank you for your support. You took simple ideas and turned them into concepts readers can implement. You forced me to communicate more effectively, think beyond the single page, and got me to share your passion for not just writing "a" book but for writing this book. You know your name belongs on the front cover along with mine.

Laurie Page and Kyle Smith, I thank you for the time you invested in reading my raw pages. I learned that, as an author, when you're *in it* sometimes you can't *see it*. Thank you for investing nights and weekends in providing feedback.

To my editor Helen Chang and the Author Bridge Media team, thank you. Your feedback was spot-on (if pointed!) and your direction was invaluable.

To my entire Bridge Group team, we did it. This was such a team effort. We grew the business 58% last year with me focused on nothing but the book... the book... the book. You made that happen. You never missed a beat, gave me the support I needed, and took The Bridge Group to a whole new level. You truly rock!

ACKNOWLEDGEMENTS

I love you Bridge Group clients. I want to thank you all for every learning experience you shared with me. Great relationships are a two way street and I learn from every interaction I have with market leaders like you.

Finally, thank you to the Inside Sales community. Thank you to all the fantastic practitioners I interviewed for this book, listed here:

Ardath Albee	Kyle Porter
Barbara Giamanco	Kyle York
Bob Perkins	Linda Flanagan
Brandon O'Sullivan	Lori Richardson
Brett Garrett	Mark Roberge
Carlos Garcia	Matt Heinz
Carlos Hidalgo	Nancy Nardin
Casey Corrigan	Natasha Sekkat
Chris Snell	Nick Hedges
Dan McDade	Peggy Budnick
David Berman	Pete Gracey
Devon McDonald	Ralph Barsi
Jamie Shanks	Ross Kramer
Jill Konrath	Scott Maxwell
John Barrows	Seth List
JosianeFeigon	Shelley McNary
Ken Krogue	Sid Kumar
Kevin Gaither	Stephen DePaoli
Kris Semb	Steve Richard
Kristy Nittskoff	Tom Murdock

I truly appreciate your time and your expertise. The community we have built together is amazing. Keep on rocking!

INDEX

Made in the USA
San Bernardino, CA
18 July 2016